Revenue Statistics in Asian Countries

1990-2013

TRENDS IN INDONESIA, MALAYSIA AND THE PHILIPPINES

Please cite this publication as:
OECD (2015), *Revenue Statistics in Asian Countries 2015: Trends in Indonesia, Malaysia and the Philippines*, OECD Publishing, Paris.
http://dx.doi.org/10.1787/9789264234277-en

ISBN 978-92-64-23425-3 (print)
ISBN 978-92-64-23427-7 (PDF)

Corrigenda to OECD publications may be found on line at: *www.oecd.org/about/publishing/corrigenda.htm*.

Foreword

Revenue Statistics in Asian Countries: Trends in Indonesia, Malaysia and the Philippines is a joint publication by the OECD Centre for Tax Policy and Administration and the OECD Development Centre. It presents detailed, internationally comparable data on tax revenues for five Asian economies, two of which (Korea and Japan) are OECD members. Its approach is based on the well-established methodology of the OECD Revenue Statistics (OECD, 2014), which has become an essential reference source for OECD member countries. Comparisons are also made with the average for OECD economies.

In this publication, the term "taxes" is confined to compulsory, unrequited payments to general government. As outlined in the Interpretative guide to the Revenue Statistics, taxes are "unrequited" in the sense that benefits provided by government to taxpayers are not normally in proportion to their payments. The OECD methodology classifies a tax according to its base: income, profits and capital gains (classified under heading 1000), payroll (heading 3000), property (heading 4000), goods and services (heading 5000) and other taxes (heading 6000). Compulsory social security contributions paid to general government are treated as taxes, and are classified under heading 2000. Much greater detail on the tax concept, the classification of taxes and the accrual basis of reporting is set out in the Interpretative Guide in Annex A.

Extending the OECD methodology to Asian countries makes possible comparisons of tax systems on a consistent basis between countries in Asia, Latin America, the Caribbean and the OECD.

The report also provides an overview of the main taxation trends in Indonesia, Malaysia and the Philippines. It examines changes in both the levels and the composition of tax revenues plus the attribution by sub-level of government between 1990 and 2013.

The report also includes a special feature which includes country profiles of tax administration and recent related reforms in Indonesia, Malaysia and the Philippines.

Acknowledgements

Revenue Statistics in Asian Countries: Trends in Indonesia, Malaysia and the Philippines is jointly produced by the Organisation for Economic Co-operation and Development (OECD) Centre for Tax Policy and Administration and the OECD Development Centre. The staff from these two entities with responsibility for producing the publication were: Kensuke Tanaka, Head of Asia Desk and Prasiwi Ibrahim, Policy Analyst at the OECD Development Centre under the supervision of Director Mario Pezzini and Deputy Director Nicola Harrington; Maurice Nettley, Head, Tax data and statistical publications and Emmanuelle Modica, Statistician, of the OECD Centre for Tax Policy and Administration under the supervision of the Director Pascal Saint-Amans, Deputy Director Grace Perez-Navarro and the Head of the Tax Policy and Tax Statistics Division David Bradbury.

The authors would like to thank other staff at the OECD Development Centre and the Centre for Tax Policy and Administration for their invaluable help in completing this publication. Elizabeth Nash and Delphine Grandrieux from the OECD Development Centre's Communications and Publications team ensured the production of the publication, in both paper and electronic form. Kojiro Yoshizawa, Deputy Head, Global Relations of the OECD Centre for Tax Policy and Administration ensured co-ordination with the Asian Development Bank. Useful inputs and comments were provided by, in particular, Derek Carnegie, Economist at the OECD Development Centre, Donghyun Park, Principal Economist and Yuji Miyaki, Public Management Specialist, both of the Asian Development Bank. Support was also provided by Rintaro Tamaki, Deputy Secretary General of the OECD as well as Gil Beltran, Kunta Nugraha, Adi Cahyadi, Syaifullah, Marhaeny Tualai, Arie Yanwar, Lim Kien Thai, Mohd Shafizan Sapie and Teresa Mendoza.

The Centre for Tax Policy and Administration and the Development Centre gratefully acknowledge financial support from the government of Japan. Finally, the authors are also very grateful to colleagues working in national governments with whom they consulted regularly. These institutions include the finance ministries of Indonesia, the Philippines, Japan, Korea and the Inland Revenue Board of Malaysia.

Table of contents

List of tables

Part I

Tax revenue trends 1990-2013

Part II

Tax levels and tax structures 1990-2013

Part III

Country tables 1990-2013 - Tax revenues

Part IV

Special feature: Country profiles of tax administration and recent related reforms

List of charts

Part I

Tax revenue trends 1990-2013

Part II

Tax levels and tax structures 1990-2013

Part IV

Special feature: Country profiles of tax administration and recent related reforms

Executive summary

Tax revenues as a proportion of national incomes in Indonesia, Malaysia and the Philippines are substantially lower than in Korea and Japan. The ratios in Indonesia, Malaysia and the Philippines ranged from 13-17% compared with 25-29% in the two OECD member countries. The OECD average was higher at 34.1%.

The Report provides internationally comparable data on tax levels and tax structures for the five Asian countries. The Report also includes a special feature with country profiles on Indonesia, Malaysia and the Philippines. It is a joint publication by the OECD Development Centre and the Centre for Tax Policy and Administration. Using the same methodology as the *OECD Revenue Statistics*, it presents cross-country comparisons between the Asian economies and OECD economies.

In this publication, "taxes" are defined as compulsory, unrequited payments to general government. Taxes are "unrequited" in the sense that benefits provided by government to taxpayers are not normally in proportion to their payments. The OECD methodology classifies a tax according to its base: income, profits and capital gains (classified under heading 1000), payroll (3000), property (4000), goods and services (5000) and other taxes (6000). Compulsory social security contributions (SSCs) paid to general government are classified as taxes under heading 2000. More information on the tax classification and the basis of reporting is set out in the Interpretative Guide in Annex A.

The second edition of the *Revenue Statistics in Asian Countries* introduces a *Special Feature*, to become a regular part of future editions, which includes country profiles of tax administration and recent related reforms in Indonesia, Malaysia and the Philippines.

Key findings

Tax to GDP ratios

- Compared to 2012, the tax burden in 2013 remained at 13.1% in Indonesia, increased by 0.4 percentage points in the Philippines to 16.2% and decreased by 0.2 percentage points in Malaysia to 16.9%.

- The corresponding increases between 2000 and 2013 were an increase of 4.5 percentage points in Indonesia, 2.3 in Malaysia and 0.5 in the Philippines.

- In Indonesia, the tax burden rose strongly from 8.6% to 12.3% between 2000 and 2002. Thereafter it has remained steady in the range of 12% to 14%.

- In Malaysia, the tax ratio was steady at around 20% between 1990 and 1997. Since then it has been lower and from 2003 onwards, it has remained in the range of 14% to 17%.

- In the Philippines, the tax ratio fluctuated between 14% and 17% in the period between 1994 and 2013. Since 2010, it has risen steadily from 14.8% to 16.2%.

Tax structures

- Tax revenues from incomes, profits and gains represent about 40% of total tax revenues in Indonesia and the Philippines and over two-thirds in Malaysia. This compares with 30% in both Japan and Korea and 34% for OECD countries.

- Revenues from corporate income tax account for 77% of income taxes in Malaysia and around 60% in Indonesia and the Philippines whereas in Japan and Korea they account for less than half the total (39% in Korea and 48% in Japan).

- Revenues from social security contributions are relatively small in Indonesia, Malaysia and the Philippines – 2% or less of the total revenues in the first two countries and 13% in the Philippines. This compared with 26% in OECD countries, 42% in Japan and 25% in Korea.

Special feature: Country profiles of tax administration and recent related reforms

Indonesia

- The work undertaken to date in modernising aspects of the tax administration, including HR Management, IT systems and audit and filing processes has resulted in significant growth in the tax revenue collected. Despite this however, Indonesia faces the challenge of addressing low rates of registration and voluntary compliance, and high rates of tax evasion. Strengthening enforcement activities and improving performance in the collection of tax arrears remain priority areas for the administration.

Malaysia

- Malaysia faces issues such as its narrow tax base and an overdependence on oil and gas revenue. The government is trying to increase the number of taxpayers filing returns. With the Self-Assessment System (SAS) for corporate taxpayers and a similar SAS system for individual taxpayers, the number of taxpayers increased gradually. The government has also put in place initiatives to educate taxpayers and enhance government services to taxpayers.

The Philippines

- The Bureau of Internal Revenue (BIR) has implemented reforms such as the adoption of a more taxpayer-focused approach that includes the simplification of the tax system and online filing options through the Electronic Filing and Payment System (eFPS). They have been effective in helping to increase government revenues to cut public debt and to improve fiscal stability. However, tax yields remain constrained by a limited tax base, numerous exemptions and loopholes, and evasion and efforts need to be made in the near term to further raise revenue on a sustainable basis.

PART 1

TAX REVENUE TRENDS 1990-2013

A. Tax ratios

The trends in the total tax revenues, including social security contributions, as a proportion of gross domestic product (GDP) in Indonesia, Malaysia and the Philippines have shown differing patterns over the past two decades. Both Chart A and Table A also show that from 2010 the countries showed differing recovery patterns following reduced tax revenues associated with the financial crisis.

Chart A. **Total tax revenues as percentage of GDP, 1990-2013**

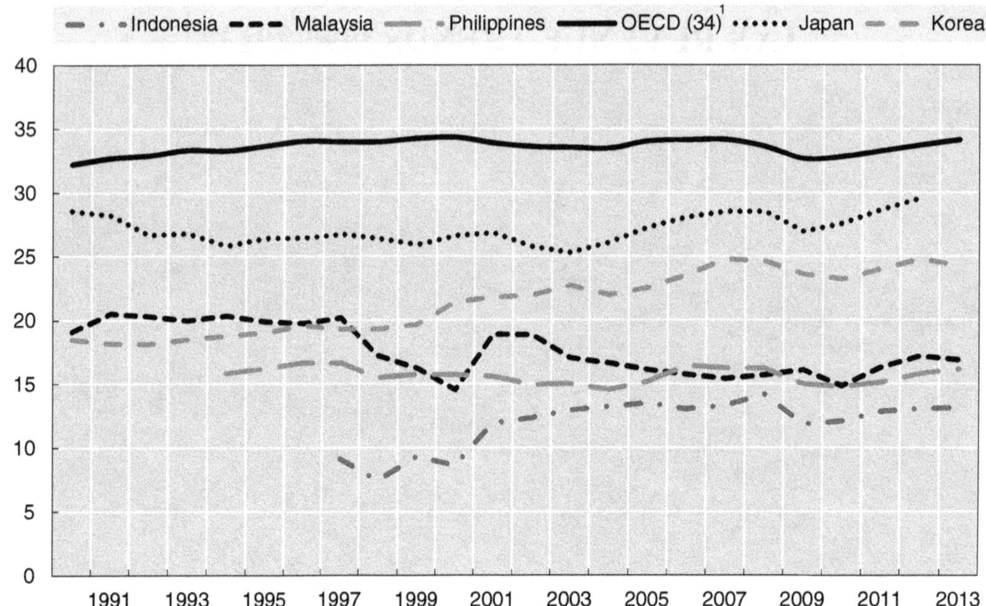

1. Represents the unweighted average for OECD member countries. Japan and Korea are also part of the OECD (34) group.

Source: Table 1 in Part II A.

StatLink http://dx.doi.org/10.1787/888933204459

Table A. **Total tax revenue as percentage of GDP**

	1990	1995	2000	2005	2008	2009	2010	2011	2012	2013
Indonesia[1]	..	..	8.6	13.5	14.2	11.9	12.1	12.8	13.1	13.1
Malaysia[2]	19.1	19.9	14.6	16.1	15.7	16.1	14.8	16.3	17.1	16.9
Philippines	..	16.2	15.7	15.2	16.2	15.0	14.8	15.1	15.8	16.2
OECD (34)[3]	32.2	33.6	34.3	34.0	33.6	32.7	32.8	33.3	33.7	34.1
Japan	28.5	26.4	26.6	27.3	28.5	27.0	27.6	28.6	29.5	..
Korea	18.5	19.0	21.5	22.5	24.6	23.6	23.2	24.0	24.8	24.3

1. The figures exclude social security contributions for Indonesia as they are not available. They are thought to be negligible as they relate only to the "Asuransi Kesehatan' – a health insurance programme for employees in for-profit state-owned enterprises.

2. The figures include local government taxes.

3. Represents the unweighted average for OECD member countries. Japan and Korea are also part of the OECD (34) group.

StatLink http://dx.doi.org/10.1787/888933204585

In Malaysia, the tax ratio of 16.9% in 2013 represented a decline of more than two percentage points compared with 1990. It remained fairly stable between 1990 and 1997 (between 19% and 20%) before falling slightly to a range of 14-19% in subsequent years. In 2010, the ratio fell to 14.8% compared to 16.1% in the previous year. It then increased in successive years to reach its highest level for the previous ten years in 2012 (17.1%).

At 13.1%, the 2013 tax to GDP ratio in Indonesia is almost 4 percentage points higher than the corresponding rate in 1997 – the first year for which firm figures are available. Indonesia saw a rising ratio in the years following 2000 which reached 14.2% by 2008 compared with around 9% in both 1997 and 2000. The upgrading of the tax administration from 2002 onwards has contributed to this increase. In 2009, there was then a sharp decline by more than two percentage points before subsequently rising again to reach 13.1% in 2013. However, in contrast with Malaysia, the 2013 figure had not reached the pre-crisis level.

In the Philippines, the ratio has been relatively stable since 1994 fluctuating between 14% and 17%. While it decreased steadily from 1996 to reach its lowest point in 2004 (14.6%), it then slowly recovered except for a decline by 1.5 percentage points during the financial crisis. For the last three years, the ratio has been increasing by around 0.5 percentage points each year on average and stood at 16.2% in 2013.

In the OECD area, the ratio has also been relatively stable – in 2013 it stood as 34.1% – just two percentage points above its level in 1990. The same was true in Japan where the ratio reached 29.5% in 2012, just one percentage point higher than in 1990. In another Asian OECD member country, Korea, the figures show an increasing trend until 2012 except for a small decline resulting from the financial crisis (the ratio rose by 6 percentage points from 18.5% in 1990 to 24.8% in 2012). It has slightly declined to 24.3% in 2013.

Tax revenues from incomes, profits and capital gains represent about 40% of total tax revenues in Indonesia and the Philippines and over two-thirds in Malaysia. Table B shows the trends in this component of revenues as a percentage of GDP.

Table B. **Taxes on income, profits and capital gains (1000) as percentage of GDP**

	1990	1995	2000	2005	2008	2009	2010	2011	2012	2013
Indonesia	..	..	4.1	6.3	6.6	5.7	5.5	5.8	5.7	5.6
Malaysia	8.2	9.2	7.7	9.4	10.3	10.6	9.4	11.1	11.9	11.6
Philippines	..	5.3	6.1	6.1	6.6	5.8	5.8	6.3	6.5	6.6
OECD (34)[1]	12.2	11.6	12.2	11.9	12.0	11.0	11.0	11.2	11.4	..
Japan	14.3	10.1	9.3	9.2	9.6	8.0	8.3	8.6	9.2	9.5
Korea	6.1	5.7	6.2	6.6	7.6	6.8	6.6	7.3	7.4	7.1

1. Represents the unweighted average for OECD member countries. Japan and Korea are also part of the OECD (34) group.

StatLink http://dx.doi.org/10.1787/888933204597

In Malaysia, tax revenues from incomes and gains as a proportion of GDP have increased by more than three percentage points since 1990 from 8.2% to 11.6% in 2013. There were several factors associated with these increases. After the 1980 economic crisis, action was taken to reduce income taxes on individuals and corporates, with the aim to promote economic growth. Certain taxes were subsequently abolished and income tax rates were lowered to almost half in addition to increased tax deductions. In the second half of the period, improved collection of revenues through changes to the tax administration added to the positive trend. The most important were more autonomy for the tax administration by making it into a statutory authority in 1996, a change in the tax collection from formal to self-assessment (2000-04), and deployment of more of the workforce to compliance programs and enforcement tasks.

As with many countries both outside and inside the OECD, income tax revenues declined following the financial crisis and this is observed in a fall of over one percentage point in 2010. However the subsequent increase took the 2011 figure above the pre-crisis levels.

In Indonesia, there has also been an increase in the income tax to GDP ratio – from 4.1% in the year 2000 to 5.6% in 2013 – but the level has remained fairly stable between 2005 and 2012 even though a fall associated with the financial crisis can still be observed.

In the Philippines, tax revenues from income, profits and capital gains as a percentage of GDP have been very stable since 1995 at around 5% to 7%. The ratios for the Philippines and Indonesia were close between 2005 and 2011 when the gap between the two countries was always 0.5 percentage points or less. Over the last four years, the Philippines' ratio has increased slowly but steadily to reach 6.6% in 2013, its highest level; whereas in Indonesia, there has been little change.

In the OECD, tax revenues from income, profits and capital gains as a percentage of GDP have been fairly stable around 11% and 12% since 1990. There was a decline of around one percentage point following the crisis and the 2012 figure is still below the corresponding 2008 level. In Japan, the contribution from this tax base declined sharply from 14.3% in 1990 to 9.3% in the year 2000 and since then the trend has been very similar to that observed in the OECD as a whole. In Korea, the trend has also been similar to the OECD average with stability around the level of 6% to 8%.

B. Tax structures

Although the overall level of the tax to GDP ratios in Malaysia has varied within a range of around six percentage points (14-20%) between 1990 and 2013, Table C2 shows that the tax structure (defined as the share of the major taxes in total tax revenue) has changed significantly. The most important of these changes relate to taxes on income and profits and consumption taxes.

- The revenues from taxes on goods and services declined steadily from 9.8% of GDP in 1990 to 3.8% in 2013 (Table 6). At the same time the share of consumption taxes in total revenues declined from 45% to 20%. This decline was faster for the specific consumption taxes as opposed to general consumption or sales taxes (largely because of the substantial falls in import and export duties).

- Over the same period, the share of tax revenues from incomes, profits and gains increased from 42.7% to 68.6%. This steadily increasing share was interrupted in 2010 as the aftermath of the financial crisis had a larger impact on the revenues from incomes and profits than those from goods and services. The upward trend resumed in 2011 and 2012.

- There is a heavy reliance on revenues from corporate income tax. They rose slightly faster than those paid by individuals. In 2013, they represented 53% of total tax revenues (Table D) and 77% of total income tax revenues.

In Indonesia, the tax "mix" remained stable between 2000 and 2013 (Table C1).

- The share of revenues from taxes on incomes, profits and gains in Indonesia showed a small decline from 48% to 42%. As with Malaysia, there is a strong reliance on corporate income tax revenues compared to those from personal income taxes – 60% of total income tax revenues were paid by corporates in 2013. However, this proportion has been in decline as the share of corporate income tax to total tax revenues fell from 30.9% to 25.9% between 2005 and 2013. The corresponding ratio for personal income tax revenues remained relatively stable at 14-17% over the same period (Table D).

- The revenues from taxes on goods and services to GDP increased from 3.9% to 5.9% over the period (Table 6). However, the proportion of revenues accounted for by consumption taxes was largely unchanged at around 45%. The share of general consumption tax revenues has increased by three percentage points since the year 2000 and at the same time the share of specific consumption taxes has fallen because the revenues from import and export taxes rose less quickly than the corresponding amounts from VAT.

The tax "mix" in the Philippines remained fairly stable between 2000 and 2013 (Table C3).

- The share of revenues from taxes on incomes, profits and gains in the Philippines has increased from 39% to 41% since 2000. About two thirds of these revenues were paid by corporates in 2013. The levels of revenues from corporate incomes and profits increased from 20.7% in 2000 to 26.1% in 2013, whereas those from individuals showed a decline of 1.5 percentage points (Table D).

- In contrast, the proportion of revenues from consumption taxes fell from 42% to 39% over the same period. The share of general consumption tax revenues increased by 3 percentage points while those for specific consumption taxes declined by 7 percentage points.

- In the Philippines, social security contributions accounted for 13% of tax revenues over the whole period.

In contrast to the Philippines, social security contributions are not an important source of government revenues in Indonesia and Malaysia. They accounted for around only 2% of revenues in Malaysia between 2000 and 2012. In Indonesia, the relevant revenue figures are not available but they are thought to be relatively small as they relate only to the "Asuransi Kesehatan" – a health insurance programme for employees in for-profit state-owned enterprises. There are no payroll taxes on the workforce in Indonesia, Malaysia or the Philippines.

In Indonesia, the share of property taxes rose from 4% to 5% of total taxation between 2000 and 2005 and then steadily fell back down to 2% in 2013. In Malaysia and the Philippines the share of this tax-type has been fairly steady and stood at around 3% in 2013.

Table C1. **Tax structures in Indonesia**[1]

	1990	2000	2005	2009	2010	2011	2012	2013
Taxes on income and profits	..	48	47	48	46	45	43	42
Social security contributions[2]	..	..	..	..	..	..	..	..
Payroll taxes	..	0	0	0	0	0	0	0
Property taxes	..	4	5	5	5	3	3	2
General consumption taxes	..	29	27	29	30	29	31	32
Specific consumption taxes	..	15	13	11	12	14	13	13
Other taxes[3]	..	4	8	7	8	9	9	10
Total	..	100	100	100	100	100	100	100

Table C2. **Tax structures in Malaysia**[1]

	1990	2000	2005	2009	2010	2011	2012	2013
Taxes on income and profits	43	53	58	66	63	68	69	69
Social security contributions	0	2	2	2	2	2	1	2
Payroll taxes	0	0	0	0	0	0	0	0
Property taxes[4]	3	3	4	4	4	3	3	3
General consumption taxes	11	12	9	7	7	6	6	6
Specific consumption taxes	34	20	20	15	17	14	14	14
Other taxes[3]	9	11	7	7	7	7	7	7
Total	100	100	100	100	100	100	100	100

Table C3. **Tax structures in the Philippines**[1]

.	1990	2000	2005	2009	2010	2011	2012	2013
Taxes on income and profits	..	39	40	39	39	42	41	41
Social security contributions	..	13	13	13	13	13	13	13
Payroll taxes	..	..	..	..	0	0	0	0
Property taxes	..	3	3	3	3	3	3	3
General consumption taxes	..	10	10	14	13	12	14	13
Specific consumption taxes	..	32	29	27	28	26	25	25
Other taxes[3]	..	4	5	4	4	4	4	4
Total	..	100	100	100	100	100	100	100

1. Represents the shares of major tax categories in total tax revenue.

2. In Indonesia, the figures for social security contributions are not available but they are thought to be negligible as they relate only to the "Asuransi Kesehatan' – a health insurance programme for employees in for-profit state-owned enterprises.

3. Including certain taxes on goods and services (headings 5130, 5200 and 5300) and other taxes (heading 6000).

4. The figures include local government taxes.

StatLink http://dx.doi.org/10.1787/888933204604

Chart B. **Tax structures in 2013**

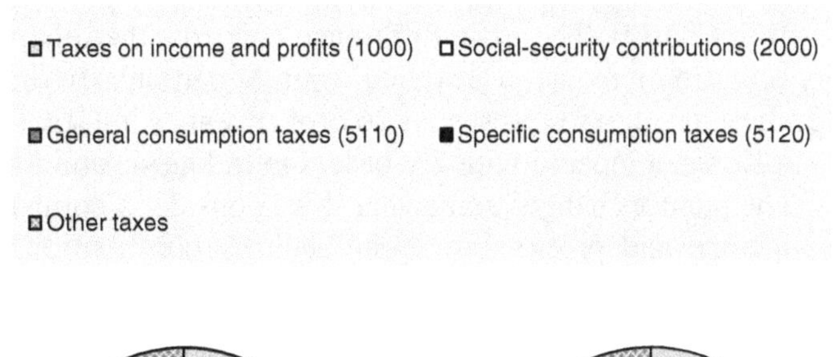

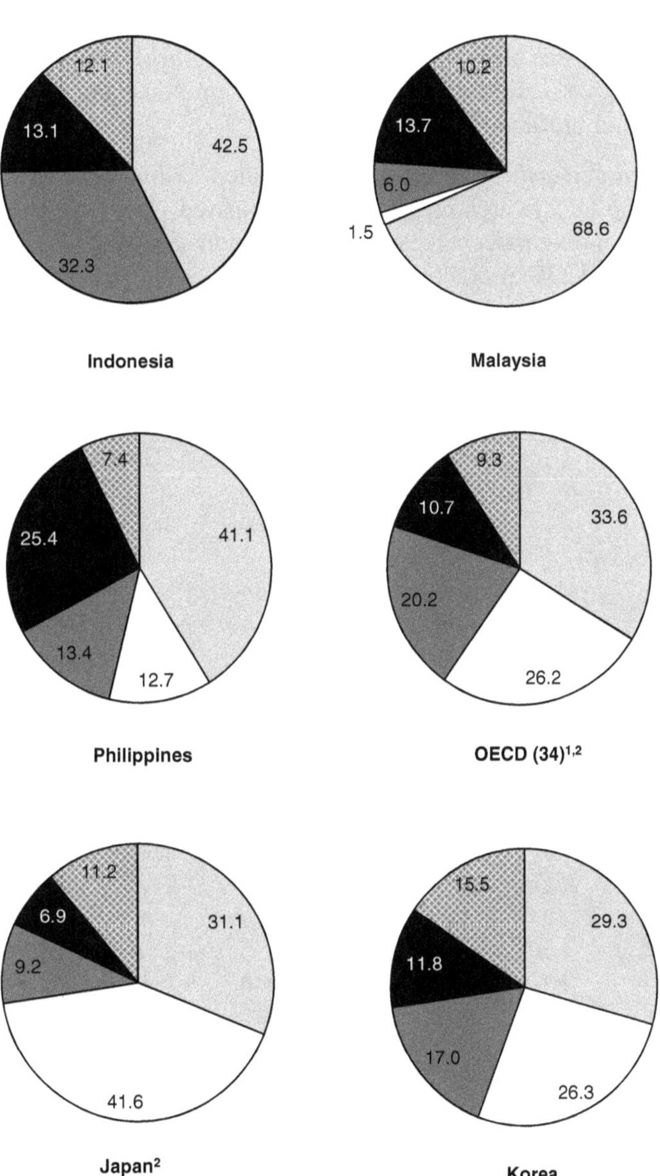

1. Represents the unweighted average for OECD member countries. Japan and Korea are also part of the OECD (34) group.

2. Data for OECD and Japan refer to 2012.

Source: Tables 2B, 7B and 8B in Part II A.

StatLink http://dx.doi.org/10.1787/888933204461

Comparing Indonesia, Malaysia and the Philippines with OECD countries and in particular with Japan and Korea, the tax structures for the latest year's available data in each case are shown in Chart B. The main difference concerns the relative unimportance of social security contributions as a revenue source particularly in Indonesia and Malaysia. In 2012, these revenues represented 26% of revenues in OECD countries, 42% in Japan and 25% in Korea compared with 2% or less in Indonesia and Malaysia and 13% in the Philippines. The picture changes somewhat if we consider a comparison of the sum of revenues from income and profits and social security contributions. This grouping accounts for as much as 70% of revenues in Malaysia, 54% in the Philippines and 43% in Indonesia compared with the OECD average of 60%, 73% of revenues in Japan and 56% in Korea. This means that the relatively small collection of social security revenues in Indonesia and Malaysia is partially offset by a higher proportion of revenues coming from taxes on incomes and profits.

Revenues from personal income taxes contributed as much as 25% of the aggregate tax collection in the OECD area in 2012. This compared with 19% in Japan and 15% in Korea. The corresponding percentages in 2013 in Indonesia, Malaysia and the Philippines were at 17%, 14% and 13% respectively.

Table D. **Taxes on income and profit as percentage of total taxation**

	1990	1995	2000	2005	2008	2009	2010	2011	2012	2013
Indonesia	..	..	47.7	46.8	46.6	47.8	45.8	45.2	43.2	42.5
Individuals	..	..	..	15.9	13.6	16.2	15.7	15.8	15.9	16.6
Corporates	..	..	..	30.9	32.9	31.6	30.2	29.4	27.3	25.9
Malaysia	42.7	46.2	52.7	58.3	65.4	65.6	63.4	67.9	69.1	68.6
Individuals	11.0	14.0	13.5	9.9	12.4	13.6	15.1	14.0	14.2	13.9
Corporates	31.4	31.4	38.4	46.8	51.3	50.3	46.6	51.7	52.8	52.8
Philippines	..	32.5	38.6	40.0	40.8	38.8	39.2	41.7	41.5	41.1
Individuals	..	11.3	14.7	13.7	12.0	11.4	12.6	13.2	13.4	13.2
Corporates	..	19.0	20.7	22.1	26.2	25.2	24.6	26.7	26.0	26.1
OECD (34)[1]	37.2	34.0	35.0	34.4	35.4	33.6	33.2	33.5	33.6	..
Individuals	29.4	25.9	25.3	23.9	24.9	24.8	24.0	24.1	24.5	..
Corporates	7.9	8.0	9.6	10.1	10.0	8.4	8.5	8.7	8.5	..
Japan	50.2	38.3	34.8	33.8	33.6	29.5	30.2	30.2	31.1	..
Individuals	27.8	22.4	21.1	18.3	19.9	20.0	18.6	18.4	18.6	..
Corporates	22.4	15.9	13.8	15.5	13.7	9.6	11.6	11.8	12.5	..
Korea	32.8	30.1	28.8	29.2	31.0	28.7	28.2	30.3	29.9	29.3
Individuals	20.0	18.1	14.6	13.3	15.0	14.2	14.3	14.8	15.0	15.4
Corporates	12.8	11.6	14.1	15.9	15.9	14.4	13.9	15.5	14.9	14.0

1. Represents the unweighted average for OECD member countries. Japan and Korea are also part of the OECD (34) group.

StatLink http://dx.doi.org/10.1787/888933204615

C. Taxes by level of government

Table E. **Attribution of tax revenues to sub-sectors of general government as percentage of total tax revenue**

	Central government			State or regional government			Local government			Social security funds		
	2000	2010	2013[3]	2000	2010	2013[3]	2000	2010	2013[3]	2000	2010	2013[3]
Federal countries												
Malaysia	94.7	94.3	95.2	..	..	..	3.4	4.0	3.3	1.9	1.7	1.5
OECD[1]	56.5	53.8	54.5	15.3	16.3	16.5	6.9	7.9	7.6	21.1	21.8	21.3
Unitary countries												
Indonesia	96.8	92.8	90.4	..	..	..	3.2	7.2	9.6	..	..	..
Philippines	81.5	82.2	82.2	..	..	..	5.3	5.2	5.2	13.2	12.7	12.7
Japan	38.7	33.0	33.7	..	..	..	26.1	25.9	24.7	35.2	41.1	41.6
Korea	68.2	60.4	58.2	..	..	..	15.1	16.7	15.5	16.7	22.8	26.3
OECD[2]	66.5	63.4	62.9	..	..	..	11.0	11.9	12.0	22.3	24.4	24.8

1. Represents the unweighted average for OECD federal member countries.

2. Represents the unweighted average for OECD unitary countries.

3. Data for OECD and Japan refer to 2012.

StatLink http://dx.doi.org/10.1787/888933204624

An analysis of tax revenues by level of government is limited by data availability in Indonesia, Malaysia and the Philippines. The available information for these three countries is compared with that for Japan, Korea and the OECD in Table E. The main conclusions are:

- The proportion of total revenues collected by local government in Malaysia and the Philippines is relatively small at around 3% and 5% respectively in 2013. In Indonesia this proportion is rising and had reached almost 10% by 2013. However, this figure is still substantially below the corresponding percentages in Japan and Korea which were 24.7% and 15.5% respectively. The corresponding average for OECD unitary countries was 12.0%.

- The trend in the share of revenues collected by local governments in OECD countries has been fairly stable since 2000. The same is true for the Asian countries covered apart from Indonesia which is currently expanding its share of revenues attributed to local governments. The proportion of total revenues collected in social security funds in Indonesia and Malaysia is negligible whereas in the Philippines it reached 13% in 2013. This compares with 41.6% in Japan, 26.3% in Korea and 24.8% for the OECD as a whole in 2013. The share of revenues from social security contributions has expanded in both Japan (by 6 percentage points) and in Korea (10 percentage points) since 2000.

D. Comparative charts

Chart C. **Total tax ratio as percentage of GDP, 2013**

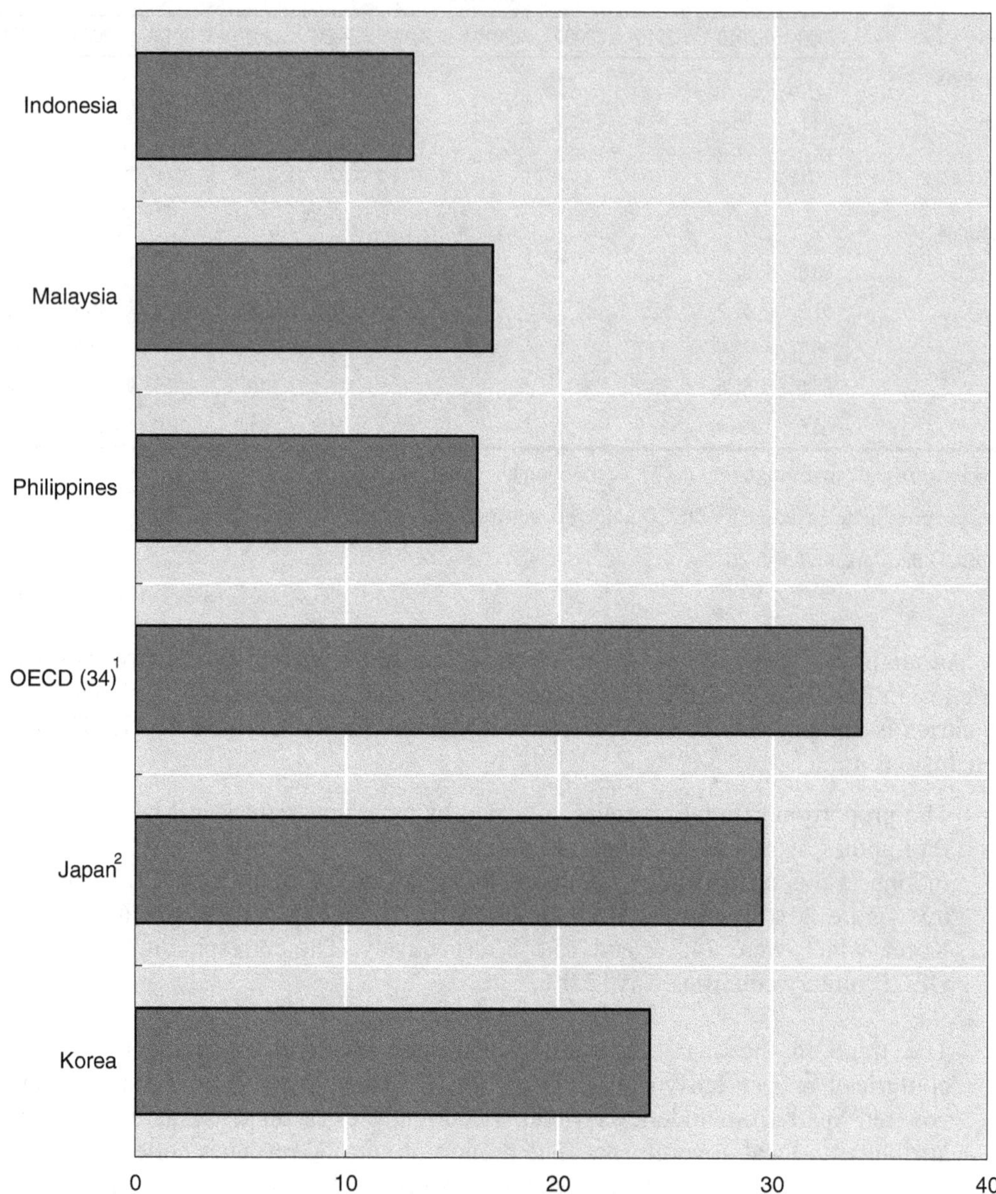

1. Represents the unweighted average for OECD member countries. Japan and Korea are also part of the OECD (34) group.
2. Data for Japan refer to 2012.

Source: Table 1 in Part II.A.

StatLink http://dx.doi.org/10.1787/888933204472

PART II

TAX LEVELS AND TAX STRUCTURES, 1990-2013

Part II

A. Comparative tables, 1990-2013

In all of the following tables ".." indicates not available or not applicable. The main series in this volume cover the years 1990 to 2013.

Table 1

Total tax revenue as percentage of GDP

	1990	1993	1994	1995	1996	1997	1998	1999	2000	2001	2002
Indonesia[1]	..	..	..	..	..	9.1	7.4	9.3	8.6	11.9	12.3
Malaysia[2]	19.1	20.0	20.4	19.9	19.8	20.2	17.2	16.3	14.6	18.9	18.9
Philippines	..	..	15.8	16.2	16.7	16.6	15.5	15.8	15.7	15.6	15.0
OECD (34)[3]	32.2	33.3	33.3	33.6	34.0	34.0	34.0	34.2	34.3	33.9	33.6
Japan	28.5	26.8	25.8	26.4	26.4	26.8	26.4	25.9	26.6	26.8	25.8
Korea	18.5	18.5	18.8	19.0	19.6	19.3	19.3	19.7	21.5	21.8	22.0

Table 1 *(cont.)*

Total tax revenue as percentage of GDP

	2003	2004	2005	2006	2007	2008	2009	2010	2011	2012	2013
Indonesia[1]	12.9	13.2	13.5	13.0	13.3	14.2	11.9	12.1	12.8	13.1	13.1
Malaysia[2]	17.0	16.6	16.1	15.7	15.4	15.7	16.1	14.8	16.3	17.1	16.9
Philippines	15.0	14.6	15.2	16.4	16.3	16.2	15.0	14.8	15.1	15.8	16.2
OECD (34)[3]	33.5	33.4	34.0	34.1	34.2	33.6	32.7	32.8	33.3	33.7	34.1
Japan	25.3	26.1	27.3	28.1	28.5	28.5	27.0	27.6	28.6	29.5	..
Korea	22.7	22.0	22.5	23.6	24.8	24.6	23.6	23.2	24.0	24.8	24.3

1 The figures exclude social security contributions for Indonesia.

2 The figures include local government taxes.

3 Represents the unweighted average for OECD member countries. Japan and Korea are also part of the OECD (34) group.

StatLink http://dx.doi.org/10.1787/888933204636

Table 2

Tax revenue of main headings

A. As percentage of GDP, 2013

	1000 Income & profits	2000 Social security[1]	3000 Payroll	4000 Property	5000 Goods & services	6000 Other
Indonesia	5.6	..	0.0	0.3	5.9	1.3
Malaysia[2]	11.6	0.3	0.0	0.6	3.8	0.7
Philippines	6.6	2.0	0.0	0.5	6.4	0.6
OECD (34)[3,4]	11.4	9.0	0.4	1.8	10.8	0.2
Japan[4]	9.2	12.3	0.0	2.7	5.3	0.1
Korea	7.1	6.4	0.1	2.5	7.5	0.7

B. As percentage of total taxation, 2013

	1000 Income & profits	2000 Social security[1]	3000 Payroll	4000 Property	5000 Goods & services	6000 Other
Indonesia	42.5	..	0.0	2.1	45.4	10.0
Malaysia[2]	68.6	1.5	0.0	3.3	22.8	3.9
Philippines	41.1	12.7	0.0	3.0	39.4	3.8
OECD (34)[3,4]	33.6	26.2	1.1	5.5	32.8	0.6
Japan[4]	31.1	41.6	0.0	9.1	18.0	0.3
Korea	29.3	26.3	0.3	10.3	30.7	3.0

1 In Indonesia, the figures for social security contributions are not available but they are thought to be negligible as they relate only to the "Asuransi Kesehatan" – a health insurance programme for employees in for-profit state-owned enterprises.

2 The figure for property tax includes local government taxes.

3 Represents the unweighted average for OECD member countries. Japan and Korea are also part of the OECD (34) group.

4 The data for OECD and Japan refer to 2012.

StatLink http://dx.doi.org/10.1787/888933204645

Table 3
Taxes on income and profits (1000)
A. As percentage of GDP

	1990	1995	2000	2005	2008	2009	2010	2011	2012	2013
Indonesia	..	..	4.1	6.3	6.6	5.7	5.5	5.8	5.7	5.6
Malaysia	8.2	9.2	7.7	9.4	10.3	10.6	9.4	11.1	11.9	11.6
Philippines	..	5.3	6.1	6.1	6.6	5.8	5.8	6.3	6.5	6.6
OECD (34)[1]	12.2	11.6	12.2	11.9	12.0	11.0	11.0	11.2	11.4	..
Japan	14.3	10.1	9.3	9.2	9.6	8.0	8.3	8.6	9.2	9.5
Korea	6.1	5.7	6.2	6.6	7.6	6.8	6.6	7.3	7.4	7.1

B. As percentage of total taxation

	1990	1995	2000	2005	2008	2009	2010	2011	2012	2013
Indonesia	..	..	47.7	46.8	46.6	47.8	45.8	45.2	43.2	42.5
Malaysia	42.7	46.2	52.7	58.3	65.4	65.6	63.4	67.9	69.1	68.6
Philippines	..	32.5	38.6	40.0	40.8	38.8	39.2	41.7	41.5	41.1
OECD (34)[1]	37.2	34.0	35.0	34.4	35.4	33.6	33.2	33.5	33.6	..
Japan	50.2	38.3	34.8	33.8	33.6	29.5	30.2	30.2	31.1	..
Korea	32.8	30.1	28.8	29.2	31.0	28.7	28.2	30.3	29.9	29.3

1 Represents the unweighted average for OECD member countries. Japan and Korea are also part of the OECD (34) group.

StatLink http://dx.doi.org/10.1787/888933204657

Table 4
Social security contributions (2000)
A. As percentage of GDP

	1990	1995	2000	2005	2008	2009	2010	2011	2012	2013
Indonesia[1]	..	..	..	..	..	..	..	..	..	..
Malaysia	0.0	0.0	0.3	0.3	0.2	0.3	0.3	0.2	0.2	0.3
Philippines	..	1.5	2.1	1.9	1.8	1.9	1.9	1.9	2.0	2.0
OECD (34)[2]	7.4	8.8	8.6	8.6	8.7	8.9	8.9	8.9	9.0	..
Japan	7.5	8.8	9.4	10.1	11.1	11.0	11.3	11.9	12.3	..
Korea	1.9	2.3	3.6	4.8	5.4	5.4	5.3	5.7	6.1	6.4

B. As percentage of total taxation

	1990	1995	2000	2005	2008	2009	2010	2011	2012	2013
Indonesia[1]	..	..	..	..	..	..	..	..	..	..
Malaysia	0.0	0.0	1.9	1.6	1.5	1.6	1.7	1.5	1.4	1.5
Philippines	..	9.2	13.2	12.5	11.4	13.0	12.7	12.7	12.9	12.7
OECD (34)[2]	22.0	25.0	24.6	25.0	25.3	26.5	26.4	26.2	26.2	..
Japan	26.4	33.5	35.2	36.9	38.8	41.0	41.1	41.5	41.6	..
Korea	10.1	12.1	16.7	21.2	21.8	22.9	22.8	23.5	24.7	26.3

1 In Indonesia, the figures for social security contributions are not available but they are thought to be negligible as they relate only to the "Asuransi Kesehatan' – a health insurance programme for employees in for-profit state-owned enterprises.

2 Represents the unweighted average for OECD member countries. Japan and Korea are also part of the OECD (34) group.

StatLink http://dx.doi.org/10.1787/888933204664

Table 5

Taxes on property (4000)

A. As percentage of GDP

	1990	1995	2000	2005	2008	2009	2010	2011	2012	2013
Indonesia	..	..	0.3	0.7	0.6	0.5	0.6	0.4	0.4	0.3
Malaysia[1]	0.6	0.5	0.5	0.6	0.6	0.6	0.6	0.6	0.6	0.6
Philippines	..	0.1	0.5	0.5	0.4	0.5	0.4	0.5	0.5	0.5
OECD (34)[2]	1.8	1.7	1.8	1.8	1.7	1.7	1.7	1.7	1.8	..
Japan	2.7	3.2	2.8	2.6	2.7	2.7	2.7	2.8	2.7	2.7
Korea	2.2	2.7	2.7	2.7	2.9	2.8	2.6	2.7	2.6	2.5

B. As percentage of total taxation

	1990	1995	2000	2005	2008	2009	2010	2011	2012	2013
Indonesia	..	..	3.7	5.2	4.4	4.6	4.7	3.1	2.7	2.1
Malaysia[1]	3.1	2.6	3.4	3.9	3.6	3.9	4.0	3.5	3.2	3.3
Phlippines	..	0.6	3.1	3.4	2.7	3.1	2.9	3.0	3.1	3.0
OECD (34)[2]	5.7	5.3	5.5	5.6	5.4	5.5	5.5	5.4	5.5	..
Japan	9.4	12.2	10.5	9.7	9.4	10.1	9.7	9.7	9.1	..
Korea	11.8	14.0	12.4	11.9	11.9	11.7	11.4	11.4	10.6	10.3

1 The figures include local government taxes.

2 Represents the unweighted average for OECD member countries. Japan and Korea are also part of the OECD (34) group.

StatLink http://dx.doi.org/10.1787/888933204673

Table 6

Taxes on goods and services (5000)

A. As percentage of GDP

	1990	1995	2000	2005	2008	2009	2010	2011	2012	2013
Indonesia	..	..	3.9	5.4	6.0	4.8	5.1	5.5	5.9	5.9
Malaysia	9.8	9.2	5.6	5.4	4.2	4.2	4.0	3.9	3.9	3.8
Philippines	..	8.7	6.6	6.1	6.6	6.2	6.1	5.9	6.1	6.4
OECD (34)[1]	10.2	11.1	11.0	11.0	10.5	10.4	10.7	10.8	10.8	..
Japan	3.9	4.2	5.1	5.3	5.1	5.1	5.2	5.3	5.3	5.3
Korea	8.2	7.7	8.2	7.7	7.8	7.6	7.9	7.5	7.7	7.5

B. As percentage of total taxation

	1990	1995	2000	2005	2008	2009	2010	2011	2012	2013
Indonesia	..	..	44.7	39.9	42.3	40.4	41.8	42.9	44.8	45.4
Malaysia	51.3	46.1	38.4	33.4	26.6	25.9	27.3	23.6	22.7	22.8
Philippines	..	53.8	42.1	39.9	40.7	41.4	41.4	38.8	38.9	39.4
OECD (34)[1]	32.9	33.8	33.1	33.2	32.1	32.5	33.1	32.9	32.8	..
Japan	13.7	15.8	19.3	19.4	17.9	19.1	18.7	18.4	18.0	..
Korea	44.3	40.7	38.4	34.3	31.6	32.0	33.9	31.4	31.2	30.7

1 Represents the unweighted average for OECD member countries. Japan and Korea are also part of the OECD (34) group.

StatLink http://dx.doi.org/10.1787/888933204680

Table 7
Taxes on general consumption (5110)
A. As percentage of GDP

	1990	1995	2000	2005	2008	2009	2010	2011	2012	2013
Indonesia	..	..	2.5	3.7	4.2	3.4	3.6	3.7	4.1	4.2
Malaysia	2.1	2.2	1.7	1.4	1.1	1.2	1.0	1.0	1.0	1.0
Philippines	..	1.4	1.5	1.5	1.8	2.1	1.9	1.9	2.2	2.2
OECD (34)[1]	5.7	6.5	6.7	6.8	6.6	6.5	6.7	6.7	6.8	..
Japan	1.3	1.4	2.4	2.6	2.5	2.6	2.6	2.7	2.7	2.8
Korea	3.5	3.4	3.7	3.9	4.0	4.1	4.1	4.1	4.3	4.1

B. As percentage of total taxation

	1990	1995	2000	2005	2008	2009	2010	2011	2012	2013
Indonesia	..	..	29.4	27.0	29.8	29.0	29.6	29.1	31.4	32.3
Malaysia	10.7	11.0	11.5	8.8	6.9	7.5	6.9	5.9	5.9	6.0
Philippines	..	8.6	9.6	10.2	11.2	14.0	13.0	12.5	13.8	13.4
OECD (34)[1]	18.1	19.5	19.7	20.2	19.8	20.0	20.5	20.4	20.2	..
Japan	4.4	5.4	9.1	9.5	8.9	9.6	9.6	9.4	9.2	..
Korea	18.7	17.8	17.0	17.4	16.1	17.3	17.6	17.1	17.2	17.0

1 Represents the unweighted average for OECD member countries. Japan and Korea are also part of the OECD (34) group.

StatLink http://dx.doi.org/10.1787/888933204692

Table 8
Taxes on specific goods and services (5120)
A. As percentage of GDP

	1990	1995	2000	2005	2008	2009	2010	2011	2012	2013
Indonesia	..	..	1.3	1.7	1.8	1.3	1.5	1.8	1.8	1.7
Malaysia	6.6	5.8	2.9	3.2	2.5	2.4	2.5	2.3	2.4	2.3
Philippines	..	7.2	5.0	4.4	4.7	4.0	4.1	3.9	3.9	4.1
OECD (34)[1]	4.0	4.1	3.7	3.6	3.3	3.3	3.4	3.4	3.4	..
Japan	2.2	2.2	2.1	2.1	2.0	2.0	2.0	2.0	2.1	2.0
Korea	4.5	3.9	4.2	3.6	3.6	3.2	3.5	2.9	3.0	2.9

B. As percentage of total taxation

	1990	1995	2000	2005	2008	2009	2010	2011	2012	2013
Indonesia	..	..	15.3	12.9	12.5	11.3	12.2	13.8	13.5	13.1
Malaysia	34.4	29.0	19.8	20.0	16.2	14.7	16.6	14.4	13.7	13.7
Philippines	..	44.6	32.0	28.9	28.9	26.7	27.6	25.6	24.5	25.4
OECD (34)[1]	13.2	12.6	11.5	11.1	10.5	10.6	10.8	10.7	10.7	..
Japan	7.5	8.3	8.0	7.7	6.9	7.3	7.2	7.1	6.9	..
Korea	24.3	20.7	19.7	15.9	14.5	13.7	15.2	12.2	12.0	11.8

1 Represents the unweighted average for OECD member countries. Japan and Korea are also part of the OECD (34) group.

StatLink http://dx.doi.org/10.1787/888933204701

Table 9

Gross domestic product for tax reporting years at market prices, in billions of national currency units

	1990	1995	2000	2005	2008	2009	2010	2011	2012	2013
Indonesia	195 597	454 514	1 389 770	2 774 281	4 948 688	5 606 203	6 446 852	7 419 187	8 230 926	9 087 276
Malaysia	119	222	356	544	770	713	797	885	942	987
Philippines	1 194	2 112	3 581	5 678	7 721	8 026	9 003	9 708	10 567	11 548
Japan	458 413	504 594	510 835	505 349	489 520	473 934	480 233	473 682	472 640	481 446
Korea	201 519	431 350	635 185	919 797	1 104 492	1 151 708	1 265 308	1 332 681	1 377 457	1 428 295

Source: National statistical offices and CEIC for Indonesia, Malaysia and the Philippines and OECD National Accounts data for Japan and Korea.

StatLink http://dx.doi.org/10.1787/888933204719

B. Comparative charts

Chart 1. **Tax revenue of main headings as percentage of total tax revenue, 2013**

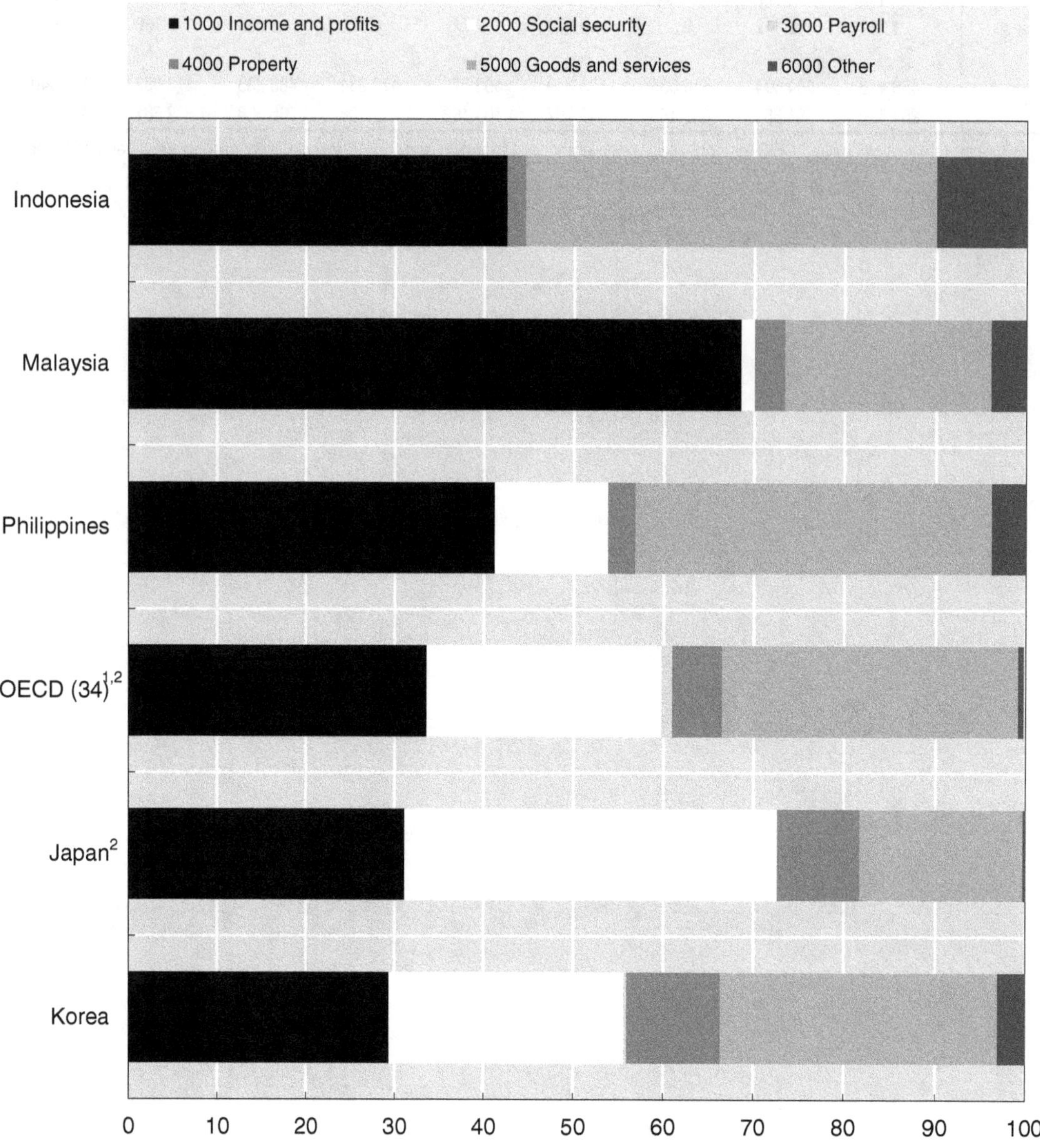

1. Represents the unweighted average for OECD member countries. Japan and Korea are also part of the OECD (34) group.
2. Data for Japan and OECD refer to 2012.

Source: Table 2B in Part II.A.

StatLink http://dx.doi.org/10.1787/888933204484

Chart 2. **Tax structures in 1990-2013**

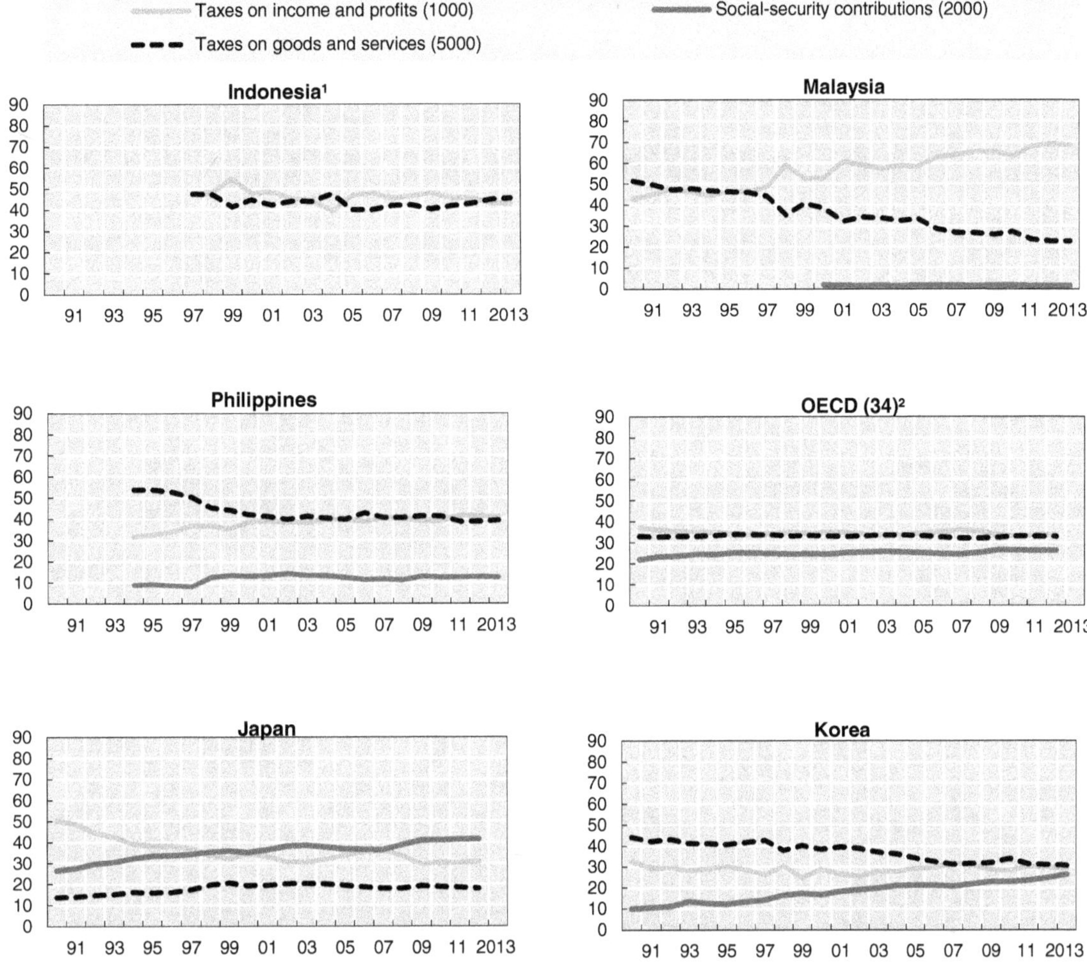

1. In Indonesia, the figures for social security contributions are not available but they are thought to be negligible as they relate only to the "Asuransi Kesehatan' – a health insurance programme for employees in for-profit state-owned enterprises.

2. Represents the unweighted average for OECD member countries. Japan and Korea are also part of the OECD (34) group.

Source: Tables 3B, 4B and 6B in Part II A.

StatLink http://dx.doi.org/10.1787/888933204496

PART III

COUNTRY TABLES, 1990-2013 – TAX REVENUES

Table 10

INDONESIA

Details of tax revenue, in billions of indonesian rupiahs (IDR)

	1990	2000	2005	2007	2008	2009	2010	2011	2012	2013
Total tax revenue	..	119 697	375 136	525 969	703 394	665 047	779 484	953 206	1 075 584	1 191 766
1000 Taxes on income, profits and capital gains	..	57 073	175 541	238 431	327 498	317 615	357 046	431 122	465 070	506 443
1100 Of individuals	..	..	59 733	77 250	96 002	107 632	122 031	150 537	171 210	197 987
1110 On income and profits	..	..	..	..	..	..	..	..	..	..
1120 On capital gains	..	..	..	..	..	..	..	..	..	..
1200 Corporate	..	..	115 808	161 181	231 496	209 983	235 015	280 585	293 859	308 456
1210 On profits	..	..	..	..	..	..	..	..	..	..
1220 On capital gains	..	..	..	..	..	..	..	..	..	..
1300 Unallocable between 1100 and 1200	..	57 073	0	0	0	0	0	0	0	0
2000 Social security contributions	..	..	..	..	..	..	..	..	..	..
2100 Employees	..	..	..	..	..	..	..	..	..	..
2110 On a payroll basis	..	..	..	..	..	..	..	..	..	..
2120 On an income tax basis	..	..	..	..	..	..	..	..	..	..
2200 Employers	..	..	..	..	..	..	..	..	..	..
2210 On a payroll basis	..	..	..	..	..	..	..	..	..	..
2220 On an income tax basis	..	..	..	..	..	..	..	..	..	..
2300 Self-employed or non-employed	..	..	..	..	..	..	..	..	..	..
2310 On a payroll basis	..	..	..	..	..	..	..	..	..	..
2320 On an income tax basis	..	..	..	..	..	..	..	..	..	..
2400 Unallocable between 2100, 2200 and 2300	..	..	..	..	..	..	..	..	..	..
2410 On a payroll basis	..	..	..	..	..	..	..	..	..	..
2420 On an income tax basis	..	..	..	..	..	..	..	..	..	..
3000 Taxes on payroll and workforce	..	0	0	0	0	0	0	0	0	0
4000 Taxes on property	..	4 456	19 649	29 677	30 927	30 735	36 607	29 892	28 969	25 305
4100 Recurrent taxes on immovable property	..	3 525	16 217	23 724	25 354	24 270	28 581	29 893	28 969	25 305
4110 Households	..	..	..	..	..	..	..	..	..	..
4120 Others	..	..	..	..	..	..	..	..	..	..
4200 Recurrent taxes on net wealth	..	0	0	0	0	0	0	0	0	0
4210 Individual	..	..	..	..	..	..	..	..	..	..
4220 Corporate	..	..	..	..	..	..	..	..	..	..
4300 Estate, inheritance and gift taxes	..	0	0	0	0	0	0	0	0	0
4310 Estate and inheritance taxes	..	..	..	..	..	..	..	..	..	..
4320 Gift taxes	..	..	..	..	..	..	..	..	..	..
4400 Taxes on financial and capital transactions	..	931	3 432	5 953	5 573	6 465	8 026	-1	0	0
Tax on Acquisition of Land and Buildings	..	931	3 432	5 953	5 573	6 465	8 026	-1	..	..
4500 Non-recurrent taxes	..	0	0	0	0	0	0	0	0	0
4510 On net wealth	..	..	..	..	..	..	..	..	..	..
4520 Other non-recurrent taxes	..	..	..	..	..	..	..	..	..	..
4600 Other recurrent taxes on property	..	0	0	0	0	0	0	0	0	0
5000 Taxes on goods and services	..	53 547	149 791	220 143	297 241	268 456	325 685	408 932	482 269	540 622
5100 Taxes on production, sale, transfer, etc	..	53 547	149 791	220 143	297 241	268 456	325 685	408 932	482 269	540 622
5110 General taxes	..	35 232	101 296	154 527	209 647	193 068	230 605	277 800	337 585	384 714
5111 Value added taxes	..	35 232	101 296	154 527	209 647	193 068	230 605	277 800	337 585	384 714
5112 Sales tax	..	0	0	0	0	0	0	0	0	0
5113 Other	..	0	0	0	0	0	0	0	0	0

Table 10 *(cont.)*

INDONESIA

Details of tax revenue, in billions of indonesian rupiahs (IDR)

	1990	2000	2005	2007	2008	2009	2010	2011	2012	2013
5120 Taxes on specific goods and services	..	18 315	48 495	65 616	87 594	75 389	95 080	131 131	144 684	155 909
5121 Excises	..	11 287	33 256	44 679	51 252	56 718	66 166	77 010	95 028	108 452
5122 Profits of fiscal monopolies	..	0	0	0	0	0	0	0	0	0
5123 Customs and import duties	..	6 697	14 921	16 699	22 764	18 105	20 017	25 266	28 418	31 621
5124 Taxes on exports	..	331	318	4 237	13 578	565	8 898	28 856	21 238	15 835
5125 Taxes on investment goods	..	0	0	0	0	0	0	0	0	0
5126 Taxes on specific services	..	0	0	0	0	0	0	0	0	0
5127 Other taxes on internat trade and transactions	..	0	0	0	0	0	0	0	0	0
5128 Other taxes	..	0	0	0	0	0	0	0	0	0
5130 Unallocable between 5110 and 5120	..	0	0	0	0	0	0	0	0	0
5200 Taxes on use of goods and perform activities	..	0	0	0	0	0	0	0	0	0
5210 Recurrent taxes	..	..	..	..	..	..	..	..	..	..
5211 Paid by households: motor vehicles	..	..	..	..	..	..	..	..	..	..
5212 Paid by others: motor vehicles	..	..	..	..	..	..	..	..	..	..
5213 Paid in respect of other goods	..	..	..	..	..	..	..	..	..	..
5220 Non-recurrent taxes	..	..	..	..	..	..	..	..	..	..
5300 Unallocable between 5100 and 5200	..	0	0	0	0	0	0	0	0	0
6000 Other taxes	..	4 621	30 155	37 718	47 728	48 241	60 146	83 260	99 276	119 397
6100 Paid solely by business	..	0	0	0	0	0	0	0	0	0
6200 Other	..	4 621	30 155	37 718	47 728	48 241	60 146	83 260	99 276	119 397
Other local level	..	3 784	28 105	34 981	44 693	45 125	56 177	79 332	95 066	114 460
Other non local level	..	837	2 050	2 738	3 034	3 116	3 969	3 928	4 211	4 937
Total tax revenue on cash basis	..	119 697	375 136	525 969	703 394	665 047	779 484	953 206	1 075 584	1 191 766

Year ending 31st December.

The data are on cash basis.

In Indonesia, the figures for social security contributions (heading 2000) are not available but they are thought to be negligible as they relate only to the "Asuransi Kesehatan' – a health insurance programme for employees in for-profit state-owned enterprises.

Source: Ministry of Finance of the Republic of Indonesia.

StatLink http://dx.doi.org/10.1787/888933204724

Table 11
JAPAN
Details of tax revenue, in billions of yen

	1990	2000	2005	2007	2008	2009	2010	2011	2012	2013
Total tax revenue	130 823	136 125	137 939	146 243	139 616	127 768	132 480	135 668	139 544	..
1000 Taxes on income, profits and capital gains	65 682	47 398	46 631	53 174	46 850	37 739	40 034	40 910	43 352	45 818
1100 Of individuals	36 394	28 677	25 222	28 600	27 790	25 518	24 663	24 951	25 946	27 119
1110 On income and profits	36 394	28 677	25 222	28 600	27 790	25 518	24 663	24 951	25 946	27 119
Income tax	25 996	18 789	16 702	16 080	14 985	12 914	12 984	13 476	14 044	15 105
Prefectural inhabitants tax	3 675	3 621	2 606	5 008	5 143	5 052	4 699	4 608	4 783	4 900
Municipal inhabitants tax	6 475	6 044	5 699	7 294	7 445	7 349	6 795	6 688	6 942	6 933
Enterprise tax	249	223	216	218	217	204	184	179	178	182
1120 On capital gains	..	..	..	..	..	..	..	..	..	..
1200 Corporate	29 288	18 721	21 408	24 573	19 061	12 221	15 372	15 959	17 406	18 699
1210 On profits	29 288	18 721	21 408	24 573	19 061	12 221	15 372	15 959	17 406	18 699
Corporation tax	18 384	11 747	13 274	14 744	10 011	6 356	8 968	9 351	10 408	11 159
Prefectural inhabitants tax	1 414	879	979	1 206	1 096	715	777	800	846	825
Municipal inhabitants tax	3 198	2 176	2 457	3 015	2 752	1 775	1 954	2 011	2 129	2 087
Enterprise tax	6 293	3 918	4 698	5 608	5 203	2 701	2 253	2 240	2 354	2 611
Local special corporate tax	0	0	0	0	0	674	1 420	1 556	1 670	2 019
1220 On capital gains	..	..	..	..	..	..	..	..	..	..
1300 Unallocable between 1100 and 1200	0	0	0	0	0	0	0	0	0	0
2000 Social security contributions	34 593	47 857	50 844	53 321	54 227	52 342	54 456	56 321	58 034	..
2100 Employees	13 883	19 786	20 980	21 972	23 250	22 484	23 590	24 431	26 871	..
2110 On a payroll basis	13 883	19 786	20 980	21 972	23 250	22 484	23 590	24 431	26 871	..
2120 On an income tax basis	0	0	0	0	0	0	0	0	0	..
2200 Employers	16 642	22 388	23 151	24 240	24 663	23 575	24 672	25 735	26 286	..
2210 On a payroll basis	16 642	22 388	23 151	24 240	24 663	23 575	24 672	25 735	26 286	..
2220 On an income tax basis	0	0	0	0	0	0	0	0	0	..
2300 Self-employed or non-employed	4 069	5 683	6 712	7 108	6 314	6 282	6 194	6 156	4 878	..
2310 On a payroll basis	4 069	5 683	6 712	7 108	6 314	6 282	6 194	6 156	4 878	..
2320 On an income tax basis	0	0	0	0	0	0	0	0	0	..
2400 Unallocable between 2100, 2200 and 2300	0	0	0	0	0	0	0	0	0	..
2410 On a payroll basis	..	..	..	..	..	..	..	..	..	..
2420 On an income tax basis	..	..	..	..	..	..	..	..	..	..
3000 Taxes on payroll and workforce	0	0	0	0	0	0	0	0	0	0
4000 Taxes on property	12 296	14 294	13 327	13 138	13 111	12 949	12 878	13 100	12 722	12 809
4100 Recurrent taxes on immovable property	7 099	10 414	10 116	9 949	10 123	10 128	10 225	10 237	9 805	9 857
Prefectural property tax	15	11	16	14	18	19	5	3	2	2
Municipal property tax	6 023	9 041	8 862	8 729	8 876	8 874	8 961	8 966	8 580	8 626
City planning tax	942	1 318	1 233	1 202	1 225	1 233	1 256	1 268	1 216	1 222
Special landholding tax	118	43	4	4	4	2	3	1	7	7
Water and land utilization tax	0	0	0	0	0	0	0	0	0	0
Land value tax	0	1	0	0	0	0	0	0	0	0
4110 Households	..	..	..	..	..	..	..	..	..	..
4120 Others	..	..	..	..	..	..	..	..	..	..
4200 Recurrent taxes on net wealth	0	0	0	0	0	0	0	0	0	0
4210 Individual	..	..	..	..	..	..	..	..	..	..
4220 Corporate	..	..	..	..	..	..	..	..	..	..
4300 Estate, inheritance and gift taxes	1 918	1 782	1 566	1 503	1 455	1 350	1 250	1 474	1 504	1 495
4310 Estate and inheritance taxes	..	..	..	..	..	..	..	..	..	..
Inheritance tax	..	..	..	..	..	..	..	..	..	..
4320 Gift taxes	..	..	..	..	..	..	..	..	..	..
Tax on gifts	..	..	..	..	..	..	..	..	..	..

Table 11 *(cont.)*

JAPAN

Details of tax revenue, in billions of yen

	1990	2000	2005	2007	2008	2009	2010	2011	2012	2013
4400 Taxes on financial and capital transactions	3 280	2 099	1 646	1 686	1 534	1 472	1 403	1 388	1 413	1 458
Bourse tax	41	0	0	0	0	0	0	0	0	0
Securities transaction	748	0	0	0	0	0	0	0	0	0
Bank of Japan note issue tax	0	0	0	0	0	0	0	0	0	0
Stamp revenues	1 894	1 532	1 169	1 202	1 088	1 068	1 024	1 047	1 078	1 102
Real property acquisition tax	596	567	477	485	445	404	379	342	336	356
4500 Non-recurrent taxes	0	0	0	0	0	0	0	0	0	0
4510 On net wealth	..	..	..	..	..	..	..	..	..	..
4520 Other non-recurrent taxes	..	..	..	..	..	..	..	..	..	..
4600 Other recurrent taxes on property	0	0	0	0	0	0	0	0	0	0
5000 Taxes on goods and services	17 917	26 227	26 786	26 256	25 060	24 364	24 730	24 966	25 056	25 426
5100 Taxes on production, sale, transfer, etc	15 647	23 180	23 722	23 241	22 111	21 561	22 160	22 410	22 592	22 993
5110 General taxes	5 778	12 350	13 135	12 841	12 443	12 221	12 675	12 745	12 902	13 298
5111 Value added taxes	5 778	12 350	13 135	12 841	12 443	12 221	12 675	12 745	12 902	13 298
5112 Sales tax	0	0	0	0	0	0	0	0	0	0
5113 Other	0	0	0	0	0	0	0	0	0	0
5120 Taxes on specific goods and services	9 868	10 830	10 588	10 400	9 668	9 340	9 485	9 665	9 690	9 696
5121 Excises	8 637	9 837	9 571	9 374	8 702	8 527	8 622	8 719	8 721	8 618
Liquor tax	1 935	1 816	1 585	1 524	1 461	1 417	1 389	1 369	1 350	1 347
Sugar excises	0	0	0	0	0	0	0	0	0	0
Local road tax	361	296	311	302	286	291	294	283	281	275
Gasoline tax	2 007	2 769	2 908	2 820	2 572	2 715	2 750	2 648	2 622	2 566
Liquefied petroleum gas tax	31	28	29	27	26	25	24	23	21	22
Aviation fuel tax	76	104	105	104	99	94	89	60	64	64
Commodity tax	5	0	0	0	0	0	0	0	0	0
Playing-card tax	0	0	0	0	0	0	0	0	0	0
Prefectural tobacco tax	361	282	275	278	263	250	256	293	289	176
Municipal tobacco tax	636	865	845	853	808	767	788	900	887	1 005
Timber delivery tax	0	0	0	0	0	0	0	0	0	0
Mineral product tax	3	2	2	2	2	2	2	2	2	2
Electricity and gas tax	0	0	0	0	0	0	0	0	0	0
Light oil delivery tax	834	1 208	1 086	1 034	919	908	918	932	925	936
Vehicle acquisition tax	613	464	453	425	366	231	192	168	210	187
Promotion of power resources development tax	295	375	359	352	341	329	349	331	328	330
Petroleum and coal tax	487	489	493	513	511	487	502	519	567	564
Tobacco tax	996	876	887	925	851	822	908	1 032	1 018	991
Special tobacco tax	0	264	233	214	197	190	163	160	158	153
5122 Profits of fiscal monopolies	0	0	0	0	0	0	0	0	0	0
Monopoly profits	..	..	..	..	..	..	..	..	..	..
5123 Customs and import duties	928	877	930	941	883	732	786	874	897	1 003
Customs duty	928	877	930	941	883	732	786	874	897	1 003
5124 Taxes on exports	0	0	0	0	0	0	0	0	0	0
5125 Taxes on investment goods	0	0	0	0	0	0	0	0	0	0
5126 Taxes on specific services	303	116	87	85	84	81	77	72	73	74
Travel tax	0	0	0	0	0	0	0	0	0	0
Admission tax	0	0	0	0	0	0	0	0	0	0
Local entertainment tax	0	0	0	0	0	0	0	0	0	0
Golf course utilization tax	90	81	62	60	60	58	55	51	51	51
Meal and lodging tax	0	0	0	0	0	0	0	0	0	0
Special local consumption tax	195	12	0	0	0	0	0	0	0	0
Bathing tax	18	23	24	25	24	23	22	21	22	23

Table 11 *(cont.)*

JAPAN

Details of tax revenue, in billions of yen

	1990	2000	2005	2007	2008	2009	2010	2011	2012	2013
5127 Other taxes on internat trade and transactions	0	0	0	0	0	0	0	0	0	0
5128 Other taxes	0	0	0	0	0	0	0	0	0	0
5130 Unallocable between 5110 and 5120	0	0	0	0	0	0	0	0	0	0
5200 Taxes on use of goods and perform activities	2 270	3 047	3 064	3 015	2 949	2 803	2 570	2 557	2 464	2 432
5210 Recurrent taxes	2 250	3 027	3 043	2 993	2 928	2 783	2 548	2 535	2 442	2 410
Automobile tax	1 276	1 765	1 753	1 717	1 681	1 654	1 616	1 597	1 586	1 571
Light vehicle tax	88	125	152	164	169	174	178	180	184	187
Motor vehicle tonnage tax	881	1 134	1 136	1 110	1 076	953	753	755	669	651
Hunter licence tax	2	2	0	0	0	0	0	0	0	0
Hunting tax	2	1	3	2	2	2	2	2	2	2
Mine lot tax	1	1	0	0	0	0	0	0	0	0
5211 Paid by households: motor vehicles	..	..	..	..	..	..	..	..	..	..
5212 Paid by others: motor vehicles	..	..	..	..	..	..	..	..	..	..
5213 Paid in respect of other goods	..	..	..	..	..	..	..	..	..	..
5220 Non-recurrent taxes	20	20	21	22	21	20	21	22	22	23
5300 Unallocable between 5100 and 5200	0	0	0	0	0	0	0	0	0	0
6000 Other taxes	335	348	351	356	367	374	381	371	386	380
6100 Paid solely by business	288	324	297	313	323	328	330	339	350	345
Business office tax	288	324	297	313	323	328	330	339	350	345
6200 Other	47	24	54	43	45	46	52	32	36	35
Taxes not in local tax law	47	24	54	43	45	46	52	32	36	35
Other	0	0	0	0	0	0	0	0	0	0
Total tax revenue on accrual basis	130 823	136 125	137 939	146 243	139 616	127 768	132 480	135 668	139 544	..

Data are on a fiscal year basis beginning 1st April.

From 1990, data are on accrual basis.

The figures for different groups of taxes are reported on different reporting bases, namely: Social security contributions (heading 2000) : in principle accrual basis, Central government taxes : accrual basis (revenues accrued during the fiscal year plus cash receipts collected before the end of May (the end of April until 1977), Local government taxes: accrual basis (due to be paid during the fiscal year and cash receipts collected before the end of May).

The Japanese authorities take the view that the Enterprise tax (classified in 1100 and 1200) and the Mineral product tax (classified in 5121) should be classified in heading 6000 since under articles 72 and 519 of the Local Tax Law these taxes are regarded as levies on the business or mining activity itself.

Heading 2000 includes some unidentifiable voluntary contributions.

Heading 2300: Includes contibutions to the National pension, National Health Insurance and the Farmer's pension fund. Contributions to or mining activity itself.

Heading 4100: Municipal property tax, includes Prefectural property tax from 1990 to 1994 because data is not available to provide a breakdown.

Heading 5121: Municipal tobacco tax, includes Prefectural tobacco tax from 1990 to 1994 because data is not available to provide a breakdown.

Heading 5121: In sub-item Petroleum and coal tax, the data before 2003 refer to petroleum tax.

Source: Tax Bureau, Ministry of Finance.

StatLink http://dx.doi.org/10.1787/888933204730

Table 12
KOREA
Details of tax revenue, in billions of won

	1990	2000	2005	2007	2008	2009	2010	2011	2012	2013
Total tax revenue	37 262	136 295	207 345	258 571	272 201	271 873	294 007	319 997	341 092	347 199
1000 Taxes on income, profits and capital gains	12 203	39 254	60 609	82 239	84 321	77 897	82 905	96 845	101 944	101 792
1100 Of individuals	7 440	19 950	27 570	43 276	40 910	38 618	42 098	47 299	51 185	53 311
1110 On income and profits	0	0	0	0	0	0	0	0	0	0
Income tax	0	0	3 127	4 682	4 659	4 762	4 425	4 896	5 152	4 889
Dividends and interest income tax	0	0	10 382	14 124	15 595	13 407	15 517	18 337	19 627	21 931
Wages and salaries income tax	0	0	2 082	2 607	2 698	2 829	2 986	3 365	3 595	3 432
Other income tax	4 723	16 128	4 607	6 151	4 078	6 117	6 369	8 300	9 938	10 901
Global income tax	938	0	0	0	0	0	0	0	0	0
Defence tax on income tax	325	0	0	0	0	0	0	0	0	0
Education tax on income tax	0	156	116	160	148	199	179	156	125	124
Rural development tax on interest, bus Inc & capgains relief	341	2 285	2 804	4 260	4 407	3 996	4 459	4 856	5 293	5 377
Inhabitant tax on income tax (local)	6 327	18 569	23 118	31 984	31 585	31 310	33 935	39 910	43 730	46 654
1120 On capital gains	1 113	1 381	4 452	11 292	9 325	7 308	8 163	7 389	7 455	6 657
Capital gains tax	1 113	1 381	4 452	11 292	9 325	7 308	8 163	7 389	7 455	6 657
1200 Corporate	4 757	19 271	33 039	38 963	43 409	39 279	40 807	49 546	50 759	48 481
1210 On profits	677	8 577	5 682	8 360	7 417	4 681	9 095	10 534	11 516	12 176
Corporation tax - Withholding	2 549	9 302	24 123	27 057	31 737	30 570	28 173	34 339	34 416	31 679
Corporation tax- Final returns	1 323	0	0	0	0	0	0	0	0	0
Defence tax on corporation tax	207	1 142	2 696	3 152	3 756	3 556	3 094	3 953	4 258	4 118
Inhabitant tax on corporation tax (local)	0	251	538	394	498	472	445	720	569	508
Rural development tax corporate income	4 757	19 271	33 039	38 963	43 409	39 279	40 807	49 546	50 759	48 481
Excess profit tax	0	0	0	0	0	0	0	0	0	0
1220 On capital gains	0	0	0	0	0	0	0	0	0	0
Capital gains tax	..	..	..	..	..	..	..	..	..	..
1300 Unallocable between 1100 and 1200	6	33	0	0	2	0	0	0	0	0
Business income tax	0	0	..	..	0	..	..	..	..	..
Real estate income tax	0	0	..	..	0	..	..	..	..	..
Defence tax on real estate & business income	0	0	..	..	0	..	..	..	..	..
Rural dev tax on bus inc & cap gains relief	0	30	..	..	2	..	..	..	..	..
Inhabitant tax before 1990 (local)	0	0	..	..	0	..	..	..	..	..
Farm land tax (local)	6	3	..	..	0	..	..	..	..	..
Inhabitant tax on farm land tax (local)	0	0	..	..	0	..	..	..	..	..
2000 Social security contributions	3 760	22 759	43 902	53 588	59 415	62 165	67 129	75 316	84 136	91 463
2100 Employees	1 464	8 578	17 632	21 773	24 236	25 527	28 039	31 758	35 518	38 342
Veterans' relief fund	0	0	0	0	0	0	0	0	0	0
Soldiers' annuity fund	0	0	0	0	0	0	0	0	0	0
Unemployment assurance	0	598	1 016	1 164	1 288	1 346	1 358	1 698	2 138	2 418
National welfare pension fund	429	4 325	7 746	9 338	9 976	10 358	11 004	11 832	12 867	13 890
Social benefit fund	0	0	0	0	0	0	0	0	0	0
Health Insurance	483	2 066	6 060	8 180	9 702	10 581	11 752	13 923	15 650	17 074
Teachers' pensions	86	279	520	581	612	621	789	940	1 222	1 077
Government employees pensions	406	1 144	2 004	2 202	2 345	2 308	2 814	3 020	3 268	3 435
Military personal pensions	60	166	286	308	313	313	322	345	373	448
2110 On a payroll basis	..	8 578	17 632	21 773	24 236	25 527	28 039	31 758	35 518	38 342
2120 On an income tax basis	..	0	0	0	0	0	0	0	0	0

Table 12 *(cont.)*

KOREA

Details of tax revenue, in billions of won

	1990	2000	2005	2007	2008	2009	2010	2011	2012	2013
2200 Employers	1 694	9 409	18 486	23 557	26 194	27 404	29 154	32 663	36 911	41 464
Ind works' insurance fund	550	1 876	3 182	4 431	4 844	4 732	4 632	4 806	5 508	5 436
Soldiers' annuity fund	0	0	0	0	0	0	0	0	0	0
Pneumoconiosis fund	0	0	0	0	0	0	0	0	0	0
Unemployment insurance	0	1 449	2 164	2 474	2 681	2 843	2 860	3 347	4 166	4 545
Veterans' relief fund	0	0	0	0	0	0	0	0	0	0
National welfare pension fund	430	4 340	7 759	9 383	10 009	10 393	11 052	11 833	12 930	13 958
Social benefit fund	0	0	0	0	0	0	0	0	0	0
Health Insurance	658	1 547	4 997	6 844	8 213	8 980	10 016	12 012	13 576	16 772
Teachers' pensions	56	197	384	425	447	456	594	665	731	753
Government employees pensions	0	0	0	0	0	0	0	0	0	0
2210 On a payroll basis	..	9 409	18 486	23 557	26 194	27 404	29 154	32 663	36 911	41 464
2220 On an income tax basis	..	0	0	0	0	0	0	0	0	0
2300 Self-employed or non-employed	602	4 772	7 784	8 258	8 985	9 234	9 936	10 895	11 707	11 657
2310 On a payroll basis	0	0	0	0	0	0	0	0	0	0
2320 On an income tax basis	602	4 772	7 784	8 258	8 985	9 234	9 936	10 895	11 707	11 657
2400 Unallocable between 2100, 2200 and 2300	0	0	0	0	0	0	0	0	0	0
2410 On a payroll basis	..	..	..	..	..	..	..	..	..	..
2420 On an income tax basis	..	..	..	..	..	..	..	..	..	..
3000 Taxes on payroll and workforce	153	258	514	619	682	681	714	803	868	981
Workshop tax on workforce (local)	124	258	514	619	682	681	714	803	868	981
Vocational training promotion fund	29	0	0	0	0	0	0	0	0	0
4000 Taxes on property	4 389	16 846	24 697	33 109	32 468	31 803	33 516	36 555	36 213	35 847
4100 Recurrent taxes on immovable property	980	3 385	5 030	9 196	9 859	8 859	9 270	9 779	10 315	10 809
Property tax (local)	227	728	2 588	3 755	4 411	4 423	4 817	7 617	8 049	8 267
City planning tax on urban real estate (local)	244	815	1 352	1 883	2 183	2 269	2 465	5	3	0
Community facilities tax (local)	86	341	446	543	589	591	650	705	766	912
Tax on excessive land holdings (local)	1	0	0	0	0	0	0	0	0	0
Tax on aggregate land holdings (local)	400	1 282	2	5	0	0	0	0	0	0
Rural dev tax on local agg land holdings tax	0	81	3	1	0	0	0	0	0	0
Tax on excessively increased land value	0	0	0	0	0	0	0	0	0	0
Comprehensive real estate tax	0	0	441	2 414	2 130	1 207	1 029	1 102	1 131	1 224
Rural dev tax on comprehensive real estate tax	0	0	91	483	428	242	208	223	228	250
4110 Households	0	0	0	0	0	0	0	0	0	0
4120 Others	22	138	107	112	118	127	101	127	138	156
Workshop tax on property (local)	22	138	107	112	118	127	101	127	138	156
4200 Recurrent taxes on net wealth	0	0	0	0	0	0	0	0	0	0
4210 Individual	..	..	..	..	..	..	..	..	..	..
4220 Corporate	..	..	..	..	..	..	..	..	..	..
4300 Estate, inheritance and gift taxes	354	989	1 873	2 842	2 777	2 431	3 076	3 333	4 021	4 290
4310 Estate and inheritance taxes	85	449	702	1 059	1 182	1 221	1 203	1 259	1 719	1 587
Inheritance tax	71	449	702	1 059	1 182	1 221	1 203	1 259	1 719	1 587
Defence tax on inheritance tax	14	0	0	0	0	0	0	0	0	0
4320 Gift taxes	269	540	1 171	1 783	1 595	1 210	1 873	2 074	2 302	2 703
Gift tax	225	540	1 171	1 783	1 595	1 210	1 873	2 074	2 302	2 703
Defence tax on gift tax	44	0	0	0	0	0	0	0	0	0

Table 12 *(cont.)*

KOREA

Details of tax revenue, in billions of won

	1990	2000	2005	2007	2008	2009	2010	2011	2012	2013
4400 Taxes on financial and capital transactions	2 960	11 935	17 796	21 071	19 832	20 513	21 170	23 443	21 877	20 748
Registration tax (local)	1 378	4 528	6 784	7 254	7 143	7 131	7 370	7 680	7 645	1 312
Registration tax	0	0	0	0	0	0	0	0	0	0
Defence tax on registration tax	0	0	0	0	0	0	0	0	0	0
Rural dev tax on local acquisition tax	0	246	471	627	635	621	632	982	853	874
Rural dev tax on local registration tax	0	66	64	143	142	169	144	2	2	1
Securities transactions tax	224	2 736	2 370	3 469	2 788	3 534	3 667	4 279	3 681	3 077
Rural dev tax on securities transaction tax	0	823	958	1 729	1 635	1 870	2 010	2 515	1 769	1 529
Acquisition tax (local)	1 165	3 148	6 649	7 261	6 916	6 644	6 825	7 361	7 326	13 318
Stamp tax	193	388	500	588	573	544	522	624	601	637
4500 Non-recurrent taxes	95	537	-2	0	0	0	0	0	0	0
Asset revaluation tax	95	537	-2	..	..	..	..	..	..	..
4510 On net wealth	..	..	..	..	..	..	..	..	..	..
4520 Other non-recurrent taxes	..	..	..	..	..	..	..	..	..	..
4600 Other recurrent taxes on property	0	0	0	0	0	0	0	0	0	0
5000 Taxes on goods and services	16 497	52 271	71 041	80 861	86 096	87 043	99 769	100 551	106 402	106 717
5100 Taxes on production, sale, transfer, etc	16 024	50 023	69 069	78 414	83 412	84 135	96 573	93 983	99 731	99 970
5110 General taxes	6 964	23 212	36 118	40 942	43 820	46 992	51 800	54 868	58 702	59 105
5111 Value added taxes	6 964	23 212	36 118	40 942	43 820	46 992	51 800	54 868	58 702	59 105
Value added tax	6 964	23 212	36 118	40 942	43 820	46 992	51 800	54 868	58 702	59 105
5112 Sales tax	0	0	0	0	0	0	0	0	0	0
Business tax	..	..	..	..	..	..	..	..	..	..
5113 Other	0	0	0	0	0	0	0	0	0	0
5120 Taxes on specific goods and services	9 059	26 811	32 951	37 472	39 592	37 143	44 773	39 115	41 029	40 865
5121 Excises	4 924	18 155	24 888	27 880	28 344	25 341	31 340	25 401	28 410	27 661
Commodity tax	0	0	0	0	0	0	0	0	0	0
Defence tax on commodity tax	0	0	0	0	0	0	0	0	0	0
Liquor tax	1 022	1 963	2 601	2 268	2 831	2 771	2 878	2 529	2 999	2 947
Defence tax on liquor tax	0	0	0	0	0	0	0	0	0	0
Education tax on liquor tax	81	516	693	580	739	713	724	644	774	764
Textile tax	0	0	0	0	0	0	0	0	0	0
Petroleum tax	0	0	0	0	0	0	0	0	0	0
Transport tax on petrol products	0	8 404	10 288	11 464	11 909	10 092	13 970	11 546	13 809	13 248
Education tax on transport tax	0	1 247	1 543	1 715	1 782	1 483	2 133	1 726	2 030	1 895
Electricity and gas tax	0	0	0	0	0	0	0	0	0	0
Special excise tax	1 912	2 985	4 399	5 161	4 499	3 642	5 066	5 537	5 336	5 484
Defence tax on special excise tax	337	0	0	0	0	0	0	0	0	0
Education tax on special excise tax	0	498	579	607	536	322	501	589	525	485
Rural development on special excise tax	0	37	45	54	47	20	24	45	56	56
Tobacco sales tax (local)	0	0	0	0	0	0	0	0	0	0
Tobacco consumption tax (local)	1 572	2 251	2 448	2 761	2 920	3 011	2 875	2 785	2 881	2 782
Motor fuel tax (local)	0	254	2 292	3 270	3 081	3 287	3 169	0	0	0
5122 Profits of fiscal monopolies	0	0	0	0	0	0	0	0	0	0
Monopoly profit	..	..	..	..	..	..	..	..	..	..
5123 Customs and import duties	3 692	5 936	6 530	7 690	9 068	9 486	11 046	11 350	10 220	11 012
Customs duties	2 765	5 800	6 317	7 411	8 776	9 169	10 666	10 990	9 816	10 562
Defence tax on customs duties	919	0	0	0	0	0	0	0	0	0
Special customs duties	0	0	0	0	0	0	0	0	0	0
Tonnage tax	0	0	0	0	0	0	0	0	0	0
Education tax on imports	7	99	173	234	246	273	336	322	375	429
Rural dev tax on customs exemptions	0	37	40	45	46	44	44	38	29	21
Previous year receipts	0	0	0	0	0	0	0	0	0	0

Table 12 *(cont.)*

KOREA

Details of tax revenue, in billions of won

	1990	2000	2005	2007	2008	2009	2010	2011	2012	2013
5124 Taxes on exports	0	0	0	0	0	0	0	0	0	0
5125 Taxes on investment goods	0	0	0	0	0	0	0	0	0	0
5126 Taxes on specific services	444	2 720	1 533	1 902	2 180	2 316	2 387	2 364	2 399	2 192
Telephone tax	262	1 457	0	0	0	0	0	0	0	0
Defence tax on telephone tax	0	0	0	0	0	0	0	0	0	0
Entertainment tax	0	0	0	0	0	0	0	0	0	0
Defence tax on entertainment tax	0	0	0	0	0	0	0	0	0	0
Entertainment tax (local)	0	0	0	0	0	0	0	0	0	0
Travel tax	0	0	0	0	0	0	0	0	0	0
Admission tax	0	0	0	0	0	0	0	0	0	0
Defence tax on admission tax	0	0	0	0	0	0	0	0	0	0
Education tax on banking & insurance	108	473	537	721	872	964	951	966	932	938
Horse race tax (local)	56	566	692	864	989	1 002	1 068	1 072	1 129	1 042
Rural dev tax on horse race tax	0	84	147	165	174	203	215	214	221	212
Butchery tax (local)	18	51	47	52	52	56	58	5	0	0
Regional development tax (local)	0	89	110	100	93	91	95	107	117	0
5127 Other taxes on internat trade and transactions	0	0	0	0	0	0	0	0	0	0
5128 Other taxes	0	0	0	0	0	0	0	0	0	0
5130 Unallocable between 5110 and 5120	0	0	0	0	0	0	0	0	0	0
5200 Taxes on use of goods and perform activities	474	2 248	1 972	2 447	2 684	2 908	3 196	6 568	6 671	6 747
5210 Recurrent taxes	474	2 248	1 972	2 447	2 684	2 908	3 196	6 568	6 671	6 747
License tax (local)	48	241	70	77	73	74	76	78	78	0
Automobile tax (local)	426	2 007	1 902	2 370	2 611	2 834	3 120	6 490	6 593	6 747
5211 Paid by households: motor vehicles	..	..	..	..	..	..	..	..	..	..
5212 Paid by others: motor vehicles	..	..	..	..	..	..	..	..	..	..
5213 Paid in respect of other goods	..	..	..	..	..	..	..	..	..	..
5220 Non-recurrent taxes	0	0	0	0	0	0	0	0	0	0
5300 Unallocable between 5100 and 5200	0	0	0	0	0	0	0	0	0	0
6000 Other taxes	259	4 907	6 582	8 155	9 219	12 284	9 974	9 927	11 529	10 399
6100 Paid solely by business	0	0	0	0	0	0	0	0	0	0
6200 Other	259	4 907	6 582	8 155	9 219	12 284	9 974	9 927	11 529	10 399
Unallocable tax revenue	0	0	0	0	0	0	0	0	0	0
Previous year tax	213	1 474	2 111	2 965	3 759	6 890	4 449	4 232	5 768	4 774
Previous year tax (local)	47	474	633	672	592	600	654	728	680	601
Unallocable defence tax	0	-3	-9	0	0	0	0	0	0	0
Education tax on local taxes	0	2 962	3 847	4 518	4 868	4 794	4 871	4 967	5 081	5 024
Total tax revenue on cash basis	37 262	136 295	207 345	258 571	272 201	271 873	294 007	319 997	341 092	347 199

Year ending 31st December.

Data are on cash basis.

Heading 2000: From 1997 the contributions to the three funds (civil servant pension fund, private school teachers pension fund and medical insurance fund) are classified as security social contributions. The reasons for the change are that the contributions either became mandatory or the fund started to be managed by public authorities in that year, thereby meeting the OECD definition of social security contributions.

Heading 2200: From 2007, this includes long-term care insurance.

Source: Ministry of Finance and Economy, Ministry of Home Affairs.

StatLink http://dx.doi.org/10.1787/888933204742

Table 13

MALAYSIA

Details of tax revenue, in millions of malaysian ringgits (MYR)

	1990	2000	2005	2007	2008	2009	2010	2011	2012	2013
Total tax revenue	22 753	51 857	87 563	102 668	120 909	114 754	118 302	144 297	161 539	166 455
1000 Taxes on income, profits and capital gains	9 719	27 339	51 040	65 671	79 032	75 269	75 058	98 018	111 676	114 113
1100 Of individuals	2 506	7 015	8 649	11 661	14 966	15 590	17 805	20 203	22 977	23 055
1110 On income and profits	2 506	7 015	8 649	11 661	14 966	15 590	17 805	20 203	22 977	23 055
1120 On capital gains	..	..	..	..	..	..	..	..	..	..
1200 Corporate	7 141	19 923	40 962	52 615	62 041	57 725	55 156	74 653	85 239	87 949
1210 On profits	7 141	19 923	40 962	52 615	62 041	57 725	55 156	74 653	85 239	87 949
Company income tax	4 497	13 905	26 381	32 149	37 741	30 199	36 266	46 888	51 288	58 175
Petroleum income tax	2 644	6 010	14 566	20 453	24 191	27 231	18 713	27 748	33 934	29 753
Offshore business activity tax	0	8	15	13	17	15	15	17	18	20
Levy on Electricity	0	0	0	0	92	280	162	0	0	1
1220 On capital gains	..	..	..	..	..	..	..	..	..	..
1300 Unallocable between 1100 and 1200	72	402	1 429	1 395	2 025	1 954	2 097	3 162	3 459	3 109
Cooperatives income tax	3	87	63	189	204	546	378	357	345	286
Withholding income tax	0	0	1 110	1 190	1 350	1 328	1 268	1 519	2 097	2 008
Other income tax	0	0	20	17	22	23	21	17	21	23
Real property gains tax	69	247	236	0	110	42	303	509	608	785
Exit levy	0	41	0	0	0	0	0	0	0	0
Windfall levy on crude palm oil	0	0	0	0	112	0	0	0	0	0
Windfal levy on crude palm kernel oil	0	26	0	0	27	0	0	0	0	0
Levy on fresh fruit bunch	0	0	0	0	199	16	127	761	388	7
2000 Social security contributions	0	990	1 382	1 690	1 835	1 867	2 008	2 172	2 326	2 518
2100 Employees	0	218	304	371	402	409	439	475	508	552
2110 On a payroll basis	..	218	304	371	402	409	439	475	508	552
2120 On an income tax basis	..	0	0	0	0	0	0	0	0	0
2200 Employers	0	772	1 079	1 319	1 433	1 458	1 569	1 697	1 818	1 966
2210 On a payroll basis	..	772	1 079	1 319	1 433	1 458	1 569	1 697	1 818	1 966
2220 On an income tax basis	..	0	0	0	0	0	0	0	0	0
2300 Self-employed or non-employed	0	0	0	0	0	0	0	0	0	0
2310 On a payroll basis	..	..	..	..	..	..	..	..	..	..
2320 On an income tax basis	..	..	..	..	..	..	..	..	..	..
2400 Unallocable between 2100, 2200 and 2300	0	0	0	0	0	0	0	0	0	0
2410 On a payroll basis	..	..	..	..	..	..	..	..	..	..
2420 On an income tax basis	..	..	..	..	..	..	..	..	..	..
3000 Taxes on payroll and workforce	0	0	0	0	0	0	0	0	0	0
4000 Taxes on property	712	1 776	3 427	4 099	4 312	4 471	4 729	5 009	5 243	5 536
4100 Recurrent taxes on immovable property	687	1 774	3 422	4 099	4 311	4 471	4 729	5 009	5 241	5 535
Quit Rent	..	..	942	1 208	1 264	1 284	1 385	1 501	1 561	1 637
4110 Households	687	1 774	2 480	2 891	3 047	3 187	3 344	3 508	3 680	3 898
Assessment tax	687	1 774	2 480	2 891	3 047	3 187	3 344	3 508	3 680	3 898
4120 Others	0	0	0	0	0	0	0	0	0	0
4200 Recurrent taxes on net wealth	0	0	0	0	0	0	0	0	0	0
4210 Individual	..	..	..	..	..	..	..	..	..	..
4220 Corporate	..	..	..	..	..	..	..	..	..	..
4300 Estate, inheritance and gift taxes	25	2	5	0	1	0	0	0	2	1
4310 Estate and inheritance taxes	25	2	5	..	1	..	..	..	2	2
Estate Duty	25	2	5	..	1	..	..	..	2	2
4320 Gift taxes	0	0	0	0	0	0	0	0	0	0
4400 Taxes on financial and capital transactions	0	0	0	0	0	0	0	0	0	0
4500 Non-recurrent taxes	0	0	0	0	0	0	0	0	0	0
4510 On net wealth	..	..	..	..	..	..	..	..	..	..

Table 13 *(cont.)*
MALAYSIA
Details of tax revenue, in millions of malaysian ringgits (MYR)

	1990	2000	2005	2007	2008	2009	2010	2011	2012	2013
4520 Other non-recurrent taxes	..	..	..	..	..	..	..	..	..	..
4600 Other recurrent taxes on property	0	0	0	0	0	0	0	0	0	0
5000 Taxes on goods and services	11 669	19 910	29 216	27 483	32 194	29 746	32 268	34 114	36 647	37 871
5100 Taxes on production, sale, transfer, etc	10 842	17 990	27 051	25 772	30 323	27 834	30 218	31 883	34 317	35 421
5110 General taxes	2 442	5 968	7 709	6 642	8 374	8 603	8 171	8 577	9 496	10 068
5111 Value added taxes	0	0	0	0	0	0	0	0	0	0
5112 Sales tax	2 442	5 968	7 709	6 642	8 374	8 603	8 171	8 577	9 496	10 068
Sales tax on local goods	1 604	3 894	5 403	4 178	4 986	5 348	4 886	4 995	5 358	5 626
Sales tax on imported goods	838	2 074	2 306	2 464	3 387	3 255	3 285	3 583	4 138	4 442
5113 Other	0	0	0	0	0	0	0	0	0	0
5120 Taxes on specific goods and services	7 820	10 245	17 511	16 897	19 584	16 822	19 624	20 765	22 184	22 756
5121 Excises	2 266	3 803	9 322	8 990	10 682	10 068	11 770	11 517	12 187	12 193
Excise duties on local goods	2 266	3 803	8 641	7 910	9 174	8 474	9 350	8 415	8 420	8 395
Excise duties on imported goods	0	0	680	1 081	1 509	1 595	2 420	3 102	3 767	3 798
5122 Profits of fiscal monopolies	0	0	0	0	0	0	0	0	0	0
5123 Customs and import duties	3 421	3 599	3 385	2 424	2 635	2 114	1 966	2 026	2 282	2 524
5124 Taxes on exports	1 970	1 032	2 085	2 322	2 779	1 152	1 810	2 081	1 968	1 930
5125 Taxes on investment goods	0	0	0	0	0	0	0	0	0	0
5126 Taxes on specific services	121	1 701	2 582	3 013	3 345	3 344	3 926	4 982	5 583	5 944
Pool betting duties and sweepstakes	0	0	0	0	0	0	0	0	0	0
Service tax	121	1 701	2 582	3 013	3 345	3 344	3 926	4 982	5 583	5 944
5127 Other taxes on internat trade and transactions	43	110	137	147	142	143	151	159	164	165
5128 Other taxes	0	0	0	0	0	0	0	0	0	0
5130 Unallocable between 5110 and 5120	580	1 777	1 831	2 233	2 365	2 409	2 423	2 541	2 638	2 597
5200 Taxes on use of goods and perform activities	827	1 920	2 165	1 711	1 871	1 912	2 050	2 231	2 329	2 450
5210 Recurrent taxes	821	1 918	2 163	1 709	1 869	1 909	2 047	2 227	2 326	2 447
5211 Paid by households: motor vehicles	821	1 909	2 147	1 688	1 799	1 856	1 992	2 183	2 283	2 407
Motor vehicle licences	821	1 909	2 147	1 688	1 799	1 856	1 992	2 183	2 283	2 407
5212 Paid by others: motor vehicles	0	9	15	20	17	17	18	5	3	3
Commercial vehicle licences	..	9	14	19	16	16	17	5	3	3
Tour vehicle licences	..	0	1	1	1	1	1	1	0	0
5213 Paid in respect of other goods	0	0	1	0	53	36	38	39	39	37
Petroleum Permits	0	0	1	0	1	1	1	1	1	0
Bank Licences Fees	0	0	0	0	53	35	37	38	39	37
5220 Non-recurrent taxes	6	2	2	3	2	2	2	4	3	2
Environment Pollution Licences	1	2	2	3	2	2	2	4	3	2
Film rental tax	5	0	0	0	0	0	0	0	0	0
5300 Unallocable between 5100 and 5200	0	0	0	0	0	0	0	0	0	0
6000 Other taxes	653	1 841	2 499	3 725	3 537	3 401	4 240	4 984	5 648	6 417
6100 Paid solely by business	0	0	0	0	0	0	0	0	0	0
6200 Other	653	1 841	2 499	3 725	3 537	3 401	4 240	4 984	5 648	6 417
Share transfer tax	1	0	0	0	0	0	0	0	0	0
Stamp duties	645	1 799	2 460	3 404	3 492	3 349	4 192	4 929	5 595	6 364
Other direct taxes	8	42	38	321	45	52	48	55	53	53
Total tax revenue on cash basis	22 753	51 857	87 563	102 668	120 909	114 754	118 302	144 297	161 539	166 455

Year ending 31st December.

The data are on cash basis.

Sources: Ministry of Finance of Malaysia, Social Security Organisation, State Government Financial Report and Local Government Financial Report.

StatLink http://dx.doi.org/10.1787/888933204757

Table 14

PHILIPPINES

Details of tax revenue, in millions of philippine pesos (PHP)

	1990	2000	2005	2007	2008	2009	2010	2011	2012	2013
Total tax revenue	..	563 803	862 728	1 120 367	1 252 798	1 204 016	1 329 263	1 467 738	1 667 404	1 866 577
1000 Taxes on income, profits and capital gains	..	217 797	344 954	453 338	511 128	467 706	521 707	612 432	691 232	767 819
1100 Of individuals	..	83 006	118 582	141 673	150 936	137 108	167 605	194 025	223 165	246 894
1110 On income and profits	..	78 229	113 549	135 504	143 285	130 074	158 325	184 076	210 645	232 725
1120 On capital gains	..	4 777	5 033	6 170	7 651	7 033	9 280	9 949	12 520	14 169
1200 Corporate	..	116 987	190 775	282 835	328 547	303 544	327 210	392 457	432 915	486 943
1210 On profits	..	114 878	189 023	280 421	325 988	298 053	323 359	387 555	422 002	476 356
1220 On capital gains	..	2 110	1 752	2 414	2 559	5 492	3 851	4 902	10 913	10 587
1300 Unallocable between 1100 and 1200	..	17 804	35 597	28 829	31 645	27 054	26 892	25 951	35 152	33 982
2000 Social security contributions	..	74 200	107 900	131 830	142 200	156 000	168 430	186 203	215 356	236 575
2100 Employees	..	..	..	..	..	..	..	..	..	..
2110 On a payroll basis	..	..	..	..	..	..	..	..	..	..
2120 On an income tax basis	..	..	..	..	..	..	..	..	..	..
2200 Employers	..	19 900	23 300	26 520	27 700	33 000	34 300	38 008	54 215	54 662
2210 On a payroll basis	..	..	..	..	..	..	..	..	..	..
2220 On an income tax basis	..	..	..	..	..	..	..	..	..	..
2300 Self-employed or non-employed	..	..	..	..	..	..	..	..	..	..
2310 On a payroll basis	..	..	..	..	..	..	..	..	..	..
2320 On an income tax basis	..	..	..	..	..	..	..	..	..	..
2400 Unallocable between 2100, 2200 and 2300	..	54 300	84 600	105 310	114 500	123 000	134 130	148 195	161 141	181 913
2410 On a payroll basis	..	..	..	..	..	..	..	..	..	..
2420 On an income tax basis	..	..	..	..	..	..	..	..	..	..
3000 Taxes on payroll and workforce	..	0	0	0	0	0	0	0	0	0
4000 Taxes on property	..	17 401	29 463	32 354	33 804	36 963	39 070	44 590	50 943	56 269
4100 Recurrent taxes on immovable property	..	14 947	25 697	27 387	29 799	31 518	31 876	36 043	39 315	41 191
Real property tax (local government)	..	14 947	25 697	27 387	29 799	31 518	31 876	36 043	39 315	41 191
4110 Households	..	..	..	..	..	..	..	..	..	..
4120 Others	..	..	..	..	..	..	..	..	..	..
4200 Recurrent taxes on net wealth	..	0	0	0	0	0	0	0	0	0
4210 Individual	..	..	..	..	..	..	..	..	..	..
4220 Corporate	..	..	..	..	..	..	..	..	..	..
4300 Estate, inheritance and gift taxes	..	480	1 017	962	1 279	1 426	1 981	2 400	3 626	3 275
4310 Estate and inheritance taxes	..	302	693	650	855	982	1 451	1 635	2 315	1 650
4320 Gift taxes	..	178	324	312	424	444	531	765	1 312	1 625
4400 Taxes on financial and capital transactions	..	1 974	2 749	4 005	2 727	4 019	5 213	6 147	8 002	11 803
Stock transactions (RA 7717)	..	1 974	2 749	4 005	2 727	4 019	5 213	6 147	8 002	11 803
4500 Non-recurrent taxes	..	0	0	0	0	0	0	0	0	0
4510 On net wealth	..	..	..	..	..	..	..	..	..	..
4520 Other non-recurrent taxes	..	..	..	..	..	..	..	..	..	..
4600 Other recurrent taxes on property	..	0	0	0	0	0	0	0	0	0
5000 Taxes on goods and services	..	237 243	344 362	456 497	510 474	498 883	549 890	568 870	648 504	735 896
5100 Taxes on production, sale, transfer, etc	..	234 202	337 155	448 164	501 894	489 850	540 595	558 770	638 148	724 888
5110 General taxes	..	53 879	87 855	145 013	140 318	168 294	173 284	183 082	229 594	250 149
5111 Value added taxes	..	53 879	87 855	145 013	140 318	168 294	173 284	183 082	229 594	250 149
5112 Sales tax	..	0	0	0	0	0	0	0	0	0
5113 Other	..	0	0	0	0	0	0	0	0	0

Table 14 *(cont.)*

PHILIPPINES

Details of tax revenue, in millions of philippine pesos (PHP)

	1990	2000	2005	2007	2008	2009	2010	2011	2012	2013
5120 Taxes on specific goods and services	..	180 323	249 300	303 151	361 575	321 556	367 312	375 687	408 554	474 739
5121 Excises	..	61 677	61 816	54 998	61 415	60 548	67 203	67 993	72 346	118 856
Alcohol products	..	12 997	17 012	18 786	19 839	20 637	21 781	22 873	23 896	33 535
Tobacco products	..	17 427	23 709	23 206	27 561	24 236	31 730	25 997	32 942	71 608
Petroleum products	..	28 297	18 709	10 036	11 380	12 772	9 832	9 963	10 159	8 503
Automobiles	..	0	0	0	0	0	0	2 026	2 935	2 542
Mineral products	..	243	251	942	660	719	1 306	6 986	2 206	2 494
Others	..	2 712	2 134	2 028	1 976	2 183	2 555	148	208	174
5122 Profits of fiscal monopolies	..	0	0	0	0	0	0	0	0	0
5123 Customs and import duties	..	95 006	154 566	209 439	260 248	220 307	259 241	265 108	289 866	304 925
5124 Taxes on exports	..	0	0	0	0	0	0	0	0	0
5125 Taxes on investment goods	..	0	0	0	0	0	0	0	0	0
5126 Taxes on specific services	..	23 639	32 919	38 714	39 912	40 701	40 868	42 587	46 342	50 958
Banks and financial institutions	..	9 538	14 892	19 434	21 086	21 937	22 857	23 514	25 338	30 199
Travel tax (CHED/NCAA)	..	1 043	1 164	1 581	1 779	1 843	1 512	1 660	1 709	1 885
Immigration tax (BID)	..	47	40	42	46	39	59	61	64	69
Others	..	13 011	16 823	17 657	17 001	16 882	16 440	17 351	19 231	18 805
5127 Other taxes on internat. trade and transactions	..	0	0	0	0	0	0	0	0	0
5128 Other taxes	..	0	0	0	0	0	0	0	0	0
5130 Unallocable between 5110 and 5120	..	0	0	0	0	0	0	0	0	0
5200 Taxes on use of goods and perform activities	..	3 041	7 207	8 333	8 580	9 033	9 295	10 100	10 356	11 008
5210 Recurrent taxes	..	3 041	7 207	8 333	8 580	9 033	9 295	10 100	10 356	11 008
TO-Motor Vehicle Users' Tax	..	3 041	7 207	8 333	8 580	9 033	9 295	10 100	10 356	11 008
5211 Paid by households: motor vehicles	..	..	..	..	..	..	..	..	..	..
5212 Paid by others: motor vehicles	..	..	..	..	..	..	..	..	..	..
5213 Paid in respect of other goods	..	0	0	0	0	0	0	0	0	0
5220 Non-recurrent taxes	..	0	0	0	0	0	0	0	0	0
5300 Unallocable between 5100 and 5200	..	0	0	0	0	0	0	0	0	0
6000 Other taxes	..	17 163	36 049	46 348	55 192	44 465	50 165	55 643	61 368	70 019
6100 Paid solely by business	..	0	0	0	0	0	0	0	0	0
6200 Other	..	17 163	36 049	46 348	55 192	44 465	50 165	55 643	61 368	70 019
Documentary Stamp Tax	..	16 170	29 431	35 147	40 054	37 484	42 629	47 879	52 455	60 356
DENR-Forest charges	..	175	84	164	147	132	239	150	204	132
Miscellaneous Taxes	..	817	3 672	7 718	10 856	2 985	2 886	2 915	3 885	3 851
Other taxes (local government)	..	0	2 863	3 319	4 136	3 864	4 412	4 700	4 823	5 679
Total tax revenue on cash basis	..	563 803	862 728	1 120 367	1 252 798	1 204 016	1 329 263	1 467 738	1 667 404	1 866 577

Year ending 31st December.

The data are on cash basis.

Source: Department of Finance of the Philippines

StatLink http://dx.doi.org/10.1787/888933204769

PART IV

SPECIAL FEATURE

COUNTRY PROFILES OF TAX ADMINISTRATION AND RECENT RELATED REFORMS

Part IV

Special feature

The second edition of the *Revenue Statistics in Asian Countries* introduces a "Special Feature" that will become a regular part of future editions. The focus of the special topic will vary in each volume. The "Special Feature" of this edition includes country profiles of tax administration and related reforms in Indonesia, Malaysia and the Philippines. Please see www.oecd.org/dev/asia-pacific/revenue-statistics-asia.htm for a discussion of tax policy issues in the three countries.

INDONESIA

Key indicators (2013):

- Fiscal deficits (% of GDP): 2.3%
- Debt-to-GDP: 26.2%
- GDP growth projection, 2015-19 (percentage change): 6.0%[1]
- Total population: 248 million (estimate)

Comparison: Debt to GDP in Indonesia and the OECD average

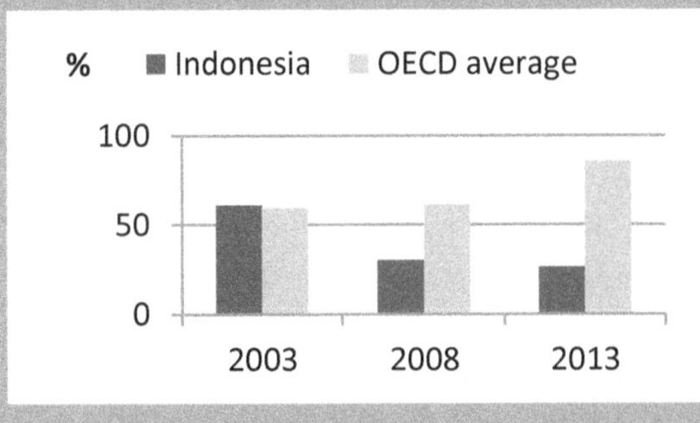

Fiscal framework:

- Annual government budget: *Anggaran Pendapatan dan Belanja Negara (APBN)*
- Fiscal ceilings: Budget deficit maximum of 3% of GDP and government debt maximum of 60% of GDP (based on State Finance Law No.17/2003). Government budget deficit 2015 target: 1.9% maximum (based on *APBN-P*).
- Public finance management: Medium Term Fiscal Framework (MTFF).

Notes:

[1]The 2015-19 projections are taken from the OECD Economic Outlook for Southeast Asia, China and India 2015.

[2]In Indonesia, the figures for social security contributions are not available but they are thought to be negligible as they relate only to the "Asuransi Kesehatan" – a health insurance programme for employees in for-profit state-owned enterprises.

[3]Including certain taxes on goods and services (headings 5130, 5200 and 5300) and other taxes (heading 6000).

[4]Unweighted average for OECD member countries. Japan and Korea are also part of the OECD (34) group.

Sources: National sources, CEIC, OECD Revenue Statistics 2014 and OECD Economic Outlook for Southeast Asia, China and India 2015.

Tax indicators:

- Tax revenues (as percentage of GDP): 13.1% (2013)
- Number of registered tax payers: 24 812 569 (2012)

Major taxes as percentage of total taxation (2013)

	%	IDR billion
Taxes on income and profits	42.50	506 443
Social security contributions[2]	-	-
Payroll taxes	-	-
Property taxes	2.12	25 305
General consumption taxes	32.28	384 714
Specific consumption taxes	13.08	155 909
Other taxes[3]	10.02	119 397
Total	100	1 191 766

Comparison: Tax structure in Indonesia (2013) and the OECD average (2012)

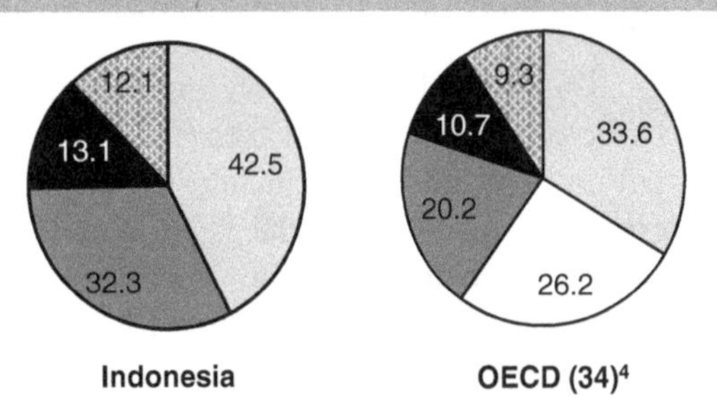

Tax administration

The number of taxpayers in Indonesia increased significantly between 2008 and 2012, partly because of tax administration reforms. The work undertaken to date in modernising aspects of the tax administration, including HR Management, IT systems and audit and filing processes has resulted in significant growth in the revenue collected. Despite this however, Indonesia faces the challenge of addressing low rates of registration and voluntary compliance, and high rates of tax evasion. Strengthening enforcement activities and improving performance in the collection of tax arrears remain priority areas for the administration.

Despite the gains made in registration and revenue collection, Indonesia still has much to do to improve the state of its tax administration. The situation it faces is made all the more challenging by the high rates of evasion. Ikhsan et al. (2005) found that Indonesia's tax reforms undertaken prior to the 21st century, while successful in increasing government revenue, were not successful in ensuring that overall revenue was either sufficient or efficiently raised. The results of their analysis showed that, at least up to 2003, there was still the opportunity to increase government revenue without having to increase tax rates. By improving the capacity of tax administration and expanding the tax base, the authors concluded, tax revenue could be increased (Ikhsan et al, 2005).

The continual decline of oil and gas revenues, partly due to the increase in oil imports as domestic oil production declined, and the considerable need for funds to support the ongoing decentralisation process as well as the economic recovery from the financial crisis have pointed to the increasing need for reforms to the tax system (Amir et al., 2013). As part of a programme to increase tax collections, the Indonesian government has introduced tax administration reforms to increase revenues, as an important part of its economic policy agenda. These reforms have been carried out in a series of initiatives that began in late 2001. In addition to targeting revenue increases, these reforms have been critically important in the government's efforts, beginning in the early 2000s, to improve the investment climate, which will be central to achieving Indonesia's growth and employment objectives (Brondolo et al, 2008).

The tax administration institution in Indonesia consists of two directorates - the Directorate General of Taxes (DGT) and Directorate General of Customs (DGC) - located within the Ministry of Finance (MOF). The DGT administers the personal income tax, the corporate income tax, the value added tax, the land and building tax and other taxes – though some are administered by regional government. Meanwhile, the DGC administers revenue from excises including tobacco, alcohol and beverages, along with revenue from international trade taxes, which consist of import and export duties. These bodies have the authority to make tax rulings, remit penalties or interest, decide on levels and mix of staff, set service standards, and influence staff recruitment criteria. Although there are two state revenue agencies under MOF, revenue from DGT contributes more than 80% of total tax revenue. Thus, the focus of tax administration policies is more towards DGT.

Indonesia, supported by the World Bank and other international donors, conducted reforms of the DGT in 2002 to address issues including weak organisational structures, poorly trained tax officials, integrity problems and large non-compliance. Through the reform, the DGT moved away from duplicative and narrowly focused tax-by-tax approaches towards function-based structures. This has enabled taxpayer segmentation based on size. Between June 2007 and 2009, the administrative reform saw the creation of high-wealth individual offices, medium taxpayer offices and small taxpayer offices (Figure 1.1).

The new organisational structure reduced the operational role of the DGT headquarters, leaving the local tax offices with the main operational tasks. The DGT headquarters functions as a policy-making body that also provides back office support to local tax offices. Human resource management has also been modernised. More intensive use of information technology has improved processes for tax filing and compliance, including simplified tax forms, electronic tax registration and filing, risk analysis, and new audit policies and procedures. The introduction or strengthening of codes of conduct, internal control units and whistle-blower protection (a "Whistleblowing System" was implemented in 2011) have improved the governance, integrity and overall reputation of the tax authorities (OECD, 2012).

Figure 1.1. **Operational Offices of the DGT organisational chart**

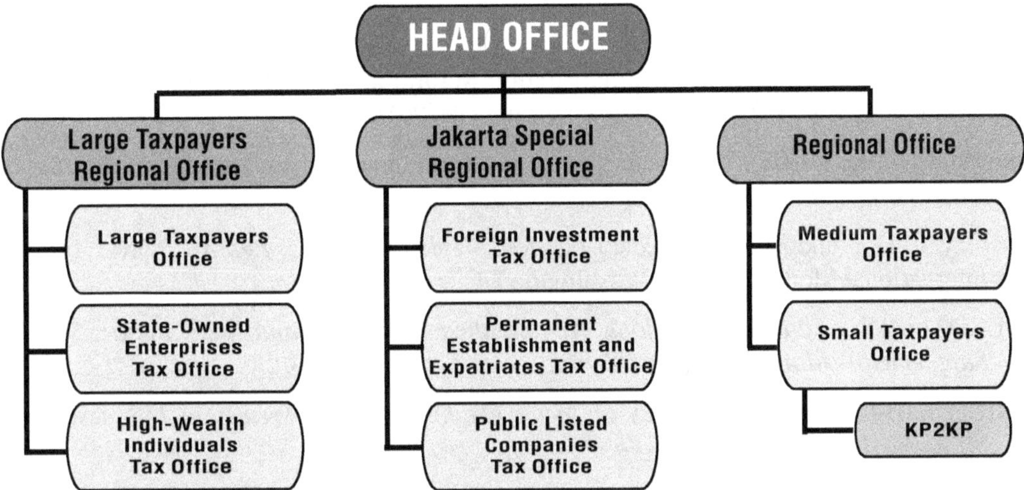

*) MTO are established only in particular Regional Offices.

Source: Pakpahan, R. (2012), "Tax reform in Indonesia: Issues, Challenges and Solutions", presentation at the IMF-Japan High Level Tax Conference for Asian and Pacific Countries on 2 February.

Overall, these measures have led to a significant improvement in tax administration performance with an estimated 1.2% of GDP of additional revenues due to improved tax collection (Brondolo et al, 2008).There has also been a significant increase in the number of registered taxpayers between 2008 and 2012 (Table 1.1).

Table 1.1. **Number of taxpayers in Indonesia (millions)**

Type of taxpayer	2008	2009	2010	2011	2012
Individual	8.81	13.86	16.88	19.88	22.13
Corporate	1.48	1.61	1.76	1.93	2.14
Government Treasurer	0.39	0.44	0.47	0.51	0.55
Total	**10.68**	**15.91**	**19.11**	**22.32**	**24.81**

Source: Directorate General of Taxes, Indonesian Ministry of Finance, 2012 Annual Report.

There is still room for improvement since tax administration reform has been slow and uneven, according to the IMF (2011). Enforcement procedures remain weak and there is low voluntary compliance. Significant weaknesses remain in the audit and arrears collection functions, which contribute to the low collection of non-oil and gas revenues (IMF, 2011)

References

Amir, H., et al (2013),"Impact of the Indonesian income tax reform: A CGE analysis", *Economic Modelling,* Vol.31.2013, 492-501.

Brondolo, J. et al (2008), "Tax Administration Reform and Fiscal Adjustment: The Case of Indonesia (2001-07)", *IMF Working Paper WP/08/129*, May.

Ikhsan, M. et al., (2005), "Indonesia's new tax reform: potential and direction", *Journal of Asian Economics 16*, 1029–1046.

IMF (2011), "Indonesia: Selected Issues", *IMF Country Reports*, No. 11/310, International Monetary Fund, Washington DC.

OECD (2015), *Economic Outlook for Southeast Asia, China and India: Special Supplement – March 2015*, OECD, Paris, http://dx.doi.org/10.1787/saeo-2015-en

OECD (2014), *Revenue Statistics in Asian Countries 2014: Trends in Indonesia and Malaysia*, OECD Publishing, http://dx.doi.org/10.1787/9789264210691-en.

OECD (2012), *OECD Economic Surveys: Indonesia 2012*, OECD Publishing, Paris, http://dx.doi.org/10.1787/eco_surveys-idn-2012-en.

MALAYSIA

Key indicators (2013):

- Federal government budget deficit (% of GDP): 4.0%
- Federal government debt (% of GDP): 54.8%
- GDP growth projection, 2015-19 (annual percentage change): 5.6%[1]
- Total population: 30 million (estimate)

Comparison: Debt to GDP in Malaysia and the OECD average

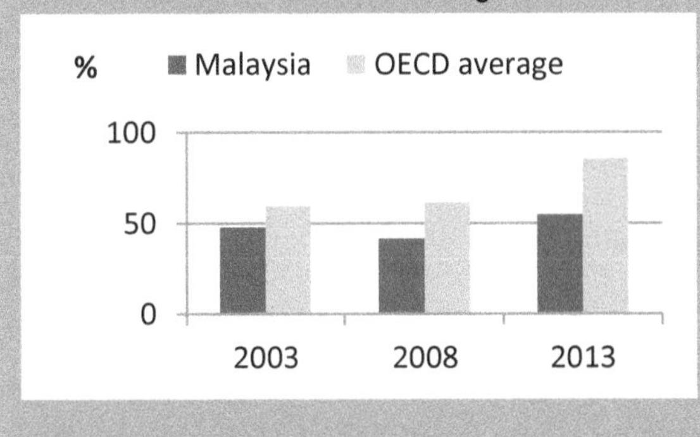

Fiscal framework:

- Federal government annual budget: *Anggaran Perbelanjaan Persekutuan.*
- Federal government domestic debt capped at 55% of GDP, measured as the sum of outstanding Malaysian Government Securities/MGS (Loan (Local) Act 1959 and Government Funding Act 1983). Federal Government budget deficit target: 3% of GDP by 2015 and near budget neutrality by 2020.
- Public finance management: Medium Term Fiscal Framework (MTFF).[5]

Notes:

[1]The 2015-19 projections are taken from the OECD Economic Outlook for Southeast Asia, China and India 2015.

[2]Includes local government taxes.

[3]Including certain taxes on goods and services (heading 5130, 5200, 5300) and other taxes (heading 6000).

[4]Unweighted average for OECD member countries. Japan and Korea are also part of the OECD (34) group.

[5]Medium Term Budget Framework (MTBF) is in the process of being developed.

Sources: National sources, CEIC, OECD Revenue Statistics 2014 and OECD Economic Outlook for Southeast Asia, China and India 2015.

Tax indicators:

- Tax revenues (as percentage of GDP): 16.9% (2013)
- Number of registered tax payers: 6 956 681 – 6 448 531 individuals and 508 150 companies (end of June 2012).

Tax structure as percentage of total taxation (2013)

	%	MYR million
Taxes on income and profits	68.55	114 113
Social security contributions	1.51	2 518
Payroll taxes	0	-
Property taxes[2]	3.33	5 536
General consumption taxes	6.05	10 068
Specific consumption taxes	13.67	22 756
Other taxes[3]	6.89	11 464
Total	100	166 455

Comparison: Tax structure in Malaysia (2013) and the OECD average (2012)

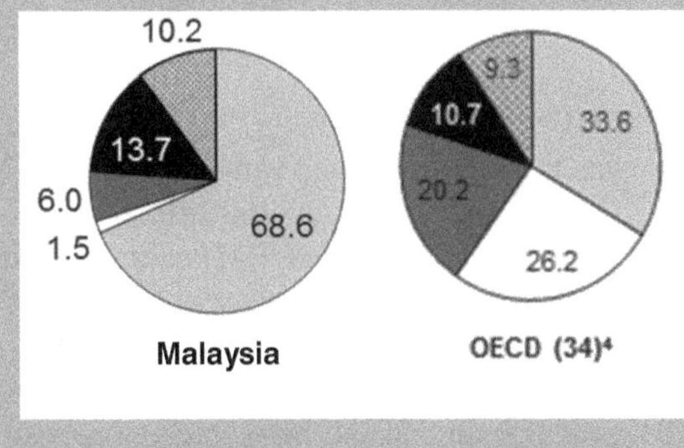

Tax administration

Malaysia remains on a trajectory towards high-income status. The country, however, needs to face issues such as its narrow tax base and an overdependence on oil and gas revenues. While taxation is obviously a fundamental source of income to fund government expenditure, it also has effects on relative prices, which in turn can influence consumption and production patterns. Malaysia has a lower tax burden when compared to most G8 and BRIC economies. It collects about 16.9% of GDP in tax revenues, compared with the OECD average of 34.1% in 2013 (OECD, 2014). Figure 2.1 below shows that Malaysia's tax to GDP ratio has been trending downwards from 1991 to 2013. The tax revenues trend in Malaysia does not show significant changes over the last ten years. There is, therefore, large room to improve tax revenue in the country.

Figure 2.1. **Tax revenues as percentage of GDP**

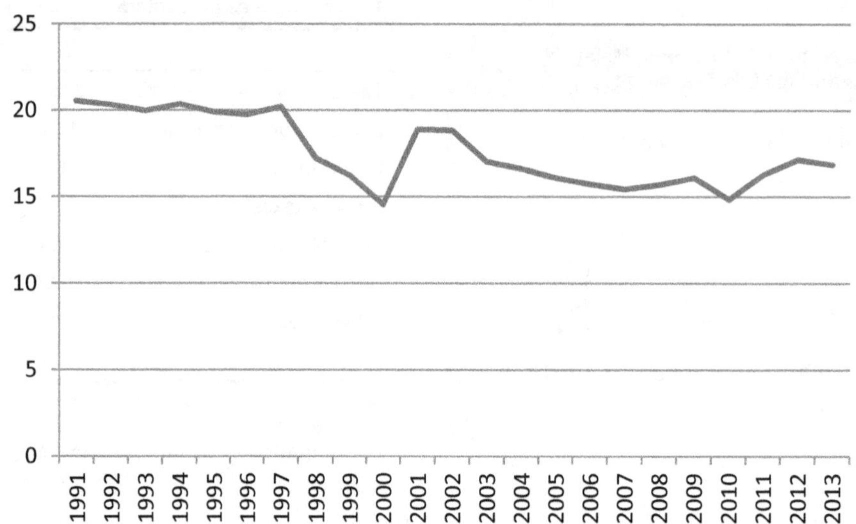

Source: Table 1 in Part II A.

StatLink http://dx.doi.org/10.1787/888933204536

Prior to March 1996, Malaysia's tax authority, the Department of Inland Revenue, was a government department under the Ministry of Finance. After that date, in order to increase the efficiency and effectiveness of the tax administration, the Inland Revenue Board of Malaysia (IRBM) was established as a separate statutory board with more autonomy and flexibility in terms of administration. With the changes, a new organisational model was implemented. The IRBM adopted a corporate governance structure with a Board of Directors to review key administration and organisational issues such as financial and human resource management (Figure 2.2).

The IRBM, among other responsibilities, acts as the government's agent in the administration, assessment, collection and enforcement of the income tax, the petroleum income tax, the real property gains tax, the estate duty, the stamp duty and other taxes agreed between the IRBM and the government (IRBM, 2013). The IRBM has the authority to make tax rulings, remit penalties/interest, design its internal structure, allocate its budget, set service standards, influence staff recruitment criteria, hire and dismiss staff, and negotiate staff pay levels (OECD, 2013).

Figure 2.2. **Inland Revenue Board of Malaysia organisational chart**

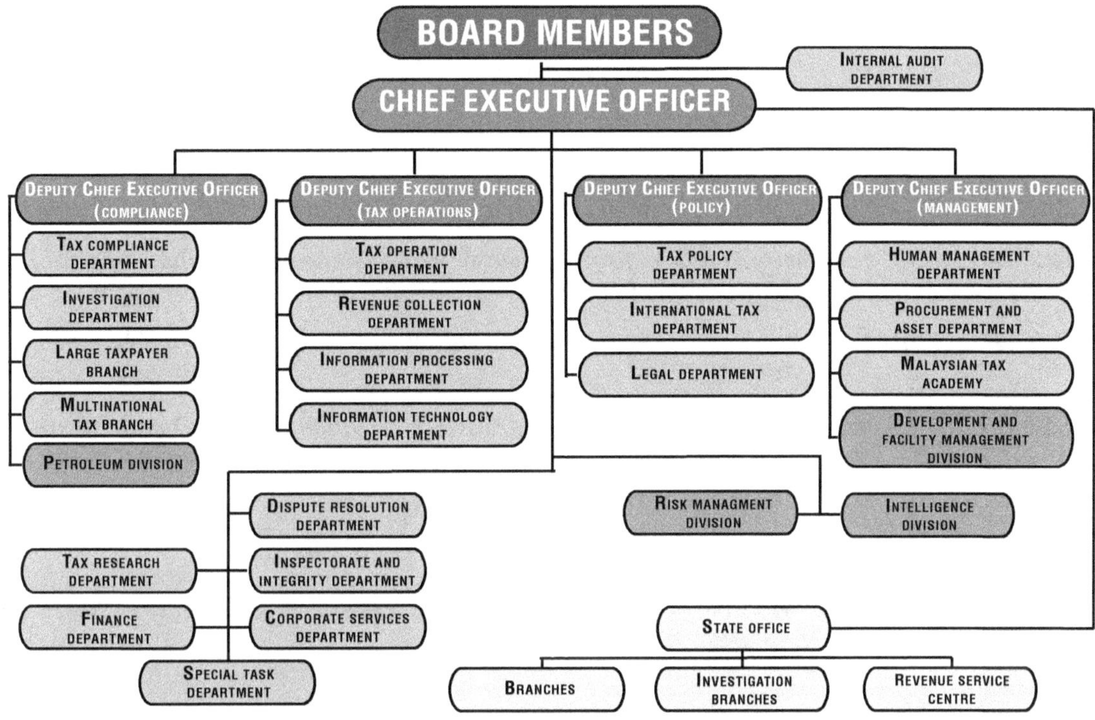

Source: Inland Revenue Board of Malaysia, www.hasil.gov.my

Prior to 2001, the IRBM assessed taxpayers by examining all tax returns they filed, a system that was administratively costly. Taxpayers' reliance on the tax authority to compute their tax liabilities fostered delays in tax collection and low voluntary compliance. In 2001, to promote voluntary tax compliance, the IRBM introduced the Self-Assessment System (SAS) for corporate taxpayers; a similar SAS system for individual taxpayers was instituted in January 2005. Under this system, taxpayers assess their own tax liability, report it and pay the tax due to the IRBM. However, despite the reforms, in 2005, the IRBM issued 3.99 million tax forms, and received only 2.72 million forms, thus 1.27 million potential taxpayers did not file their tax returns.

The success of the SAS depends not only on the co-operation of taxpayers but also on their tax literacy. The IRBM has put in place initiatives to educate taxpayers via awareness programmes, pamphlets, publications, seminars and field visits. It has also taken steps to enhance taxpayer services and to improve taxpayers' access to information to increase the number of taxpayers (Table 2.1).

Table 2.1. **Number of taxpayers in Malaysia (millions)**

Type of taxpayer	2010	2011	2012
Individual	5.45	5.47	5.79
Societies and various trust bodies	0.59	0.64	0.66
Corporate	0.45	0.47	0.51
Total	6.49	6.57	6.96

Source: Inland Revenue Board of Malaysia.

References

IRBM (2013), *Annual Report 2012*, Inland Revenue Board of Malaysia.

OECD (2015), *Economic Outlook for Southeast Asia, China and India: Special Supplement – March 2015*, OECD Publishing. http://dx.doi.org/10.1787/saeo-2015-en.

OECD (2014), *Revenue Statistics 1965-2013*, OECD Publishing. http://dx.doi.org/10.1787/10.1787/rev_stats-2012-en-fr.

OECD (2013), *Tax Administration 2013: Comparative Information on OECD and Other Advanced and Emerging Economies*, OECD Publishing. http://dx.doi.org/10.1787/9789264200814-en.

PHILIPPINES

Key indicators (2013):

- Fiscal deficit (% of GDP): 1.4%
- Debt-to-GDP: 39.2%
- GDP growth projection 2015-19 (percentage change): 6.2%[1]
- Total population: 97.6 million

Comparison: Debt to GDP in the Philippines and the OECD average

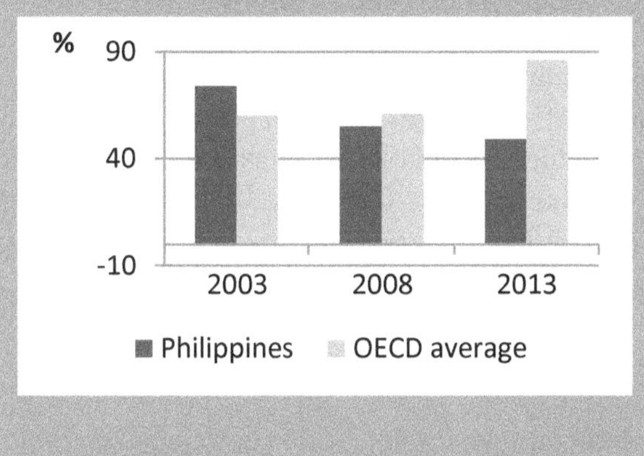

Fiscal framework - TBD

- Annual government budget: *General Appropriations Act*
- Fiscal ceilings: Budget deficit target of 2% of GDP
- Public finance management: Medium-Term Fiscal Framework (MTFF).

Notes:

[1]The 2015-19 projections are taken from the OECD Economic Outlook for Southeast Asia, China and India 2015.

[2]Includes local government taxes.

[3]Including certain taxes on goods and services (heading 5130, 5200, 5300) and other taxes (heading 6000).

[4]Unweighted average for OECD member countries. Japan and Korea are also part of the OECD (34) group.

Sources: National sources, CEIC, OECD Revenue Statistics 2014 and OECD Economic Outlook for Southeast Asia, China and India 2015.

Tax indicators:

- Tax revenues (as percentage of GDP): 16.2% (2013)
- Number of registered taxpayers: 22 989 825 (2013)

Major taxes as percentage of total taxation (2013)

	%	Million pesos
Taxes on income and profits[2]	41.14	767 819
Social security contributions	12.67	236 575
Payroll taxes	0	-
Property taxes[2]	3.01	56 269
General consumption taxes	13.40	250 149
Specific consumption taxes	25.43	474 739
Other taxes[3]	4.34	81 027
Total	100	1 866 577

Comparison: Tax structure in Philippines (2013) and the OECD average (2012)

Taxes on income and profits (1000) Social-security contributions (2000) General consumption taxes (5110) Specific consumption taxes (5120) Other taxes

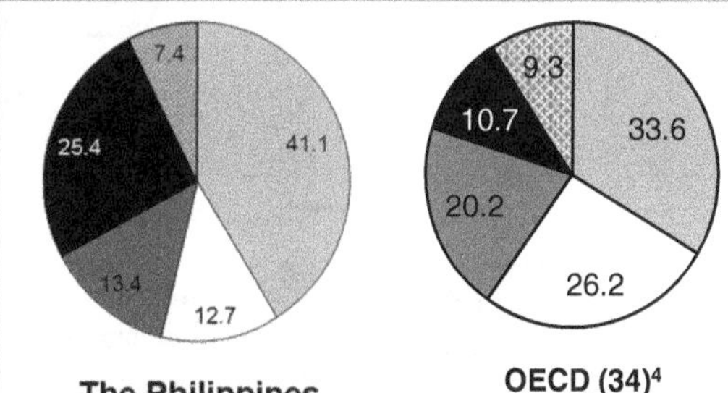

The Philippines **OECD (34)[4]**

Tax administration

Gradual reform and improvements in tax administration in the Philippines have been effective in helping to increase government revenues to cut public debt and to improve fiscal stability. Nevertheless, efforts need to be made in the near term to further raise revenue on a sustainable basis.

Tax administration in the Philippines is primarily the responsibility of the Bureau of Internal Revenue (BIR), an agency under the Department of Finance. While significant improvements have been made to the tax administration in the recent past, tax yields remain constrained by a limited tax base, numerous exemptions and loopholes, and evasion.

Historically, most tax reform efforts in the Philippines, beginning in the 1970s, have been of limited success, held back by lukewarm political support and opposition from vested interests in the bureaucracy. Deeper political economy factors have been cited as factors inhibiting broader reform of the tax system (OECD, 2015).

Despite these constraints, more recently some modernising reforms to tax administration in the Philippines have been implemented to facilitate compliance by taxpayers and to improve bureaucratic efficiency within the BIR. A major reorganisation within the agency came in 2000 with the creation of the Large Taxpayers Service, an office headed by an Assistant Commissioner and dedicated to collecting taxes from the major taxpayers that account for a large share of total revenues (Figure 3.1). However, despite this reform, these large firms remain an underutilised revenue source.

Figure 3.1. **Bureau of Internal Revenue organisational chart**

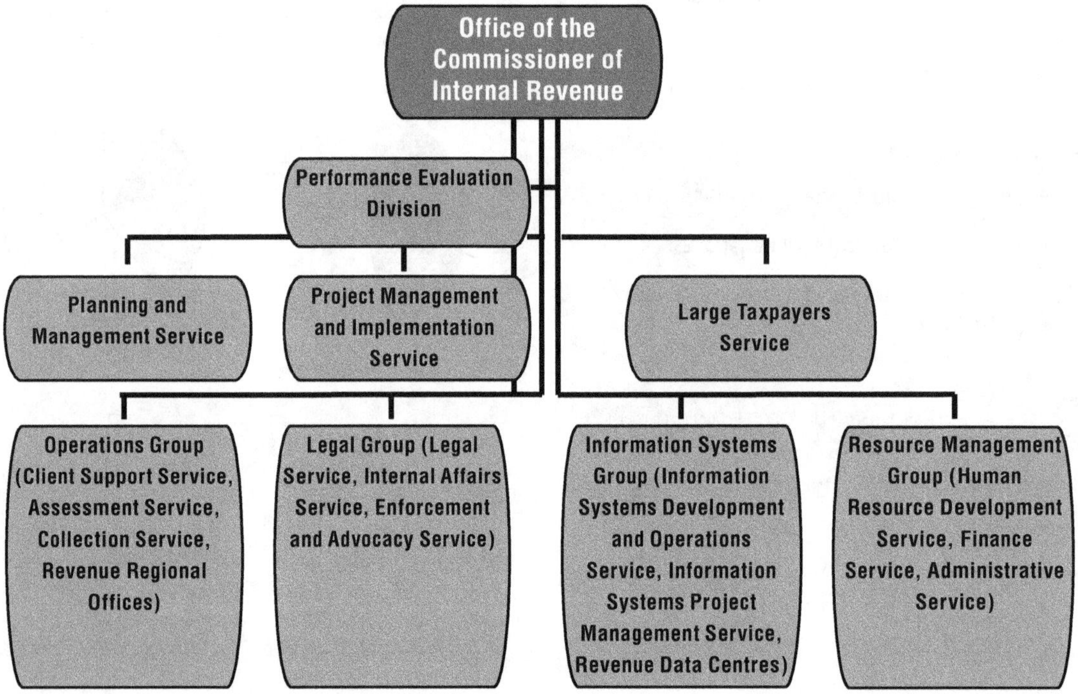

Office of the Commissioner of Internal Revenue

Performance Evaluation Division

Planning and Management Service

Project Management and Implementation Service

Large Taxpayers Service

Operations Group (Client Support Service, Assessment Service, Collection Service, Revenue Regional Offices)

Legal Group (Legal Service, Internal Affairs Service, Enforcement and Advocacy Service)

Information Systems Group (Information Systems Development and Operations Service, Information Systems Project Management Service, Revenue Data Centres)

Resource Management Group (Human Resource Development Service, Finance Service, Administrative Service)

Source: Bureau of Internal Revenue, www.bir.gov.ph.

Recent reforms to the BIR have included the adoption of a more taxpayer-focused approach that includes the simplification of the tax system and online filing options through the Electronic Filing and Payment System (eFPS) that has been available since 2001. In addition, the BIR has instituted programmes to address evasion and non-compliance, such as RATE (Run After Tax Evaders), which targets high-profile evaders through media campaigns, and the Stop-Filer Programme, which flags taxpayers that have filed in the past and then stopped. These and other initiatives have contributed to a 71% increase in the number of registered taxpayers in the Philippines in the six years between 2007 and 2013 (Table 3.1). This growth was particularly assisted by the implementation of Executive Order No. 98, signed by the former President in 1999, requiring the inclusion of Tax Identification Numbers in applications for permits, licenses and other official documents. However, this increase in registration has not been accompanied by a similar increase in tax revenues.

Table 3.1. **Number of registered taxpayers in the Philippines (millions)**

Type of taxpayer	2007	2008	2009	2010	2011	2012	2013
Corporate	0.49	0.53	0.56	0.60	0.62	0.67	0.72
Individual	9.20	10.08	10.47	11.20	12.08	13.08	14.31
Estate & Trust	0.03	0.03	0.02	0.03	0.03	0.03	0.03
Marginal Income Earners	0.16	0.17	0.10	0.11	0.12	0.12	0.12
One Time Taxpayer (ONETT)	1.96	2.20	2.14	2.34	2.60	2.83	3.07
Others (Executive Order No, 98)	1.64	1.96	2.53	3.02	3.52	4.10	4.75
Total	13.47	14.97	15.83	17.29	18.96	20.83	22.99

Source: Bureau of Internal Revenue, www.bir.gov.ph.

References

OECD (2015), *Economic Outlook for Southeast Asia, China and India 2015*, OECD Publishing, Paris http://dx.doi.org/10.1787/saeo-2015-en.

ANNEX A

The OECD Classification of Taxes and Interpretative Guide

Table of contents

Page

The OECD Classification of Taxes

1000 *Taxes on income, profits and capital gains*

- 1100 Individuals
  - 1110 Income and profits
  - 1120 Capital gains
- 1200 Corporates
  - 1210 Income and profits
  - 1220 Capital gains
- 1300 Unallocable as between 1100 and 1200

2000 *Social security contributions*

- 2100 Employees
- 2200 Employers
- 2300 Self-employed, non-employed
- 2400 Unallocable as between 2100, 2200 and 2300

3000 *Taxes on payroll and workforce*

4000 *Taxes on property*

- 4100 Recurrent taxes on immovable property
  - 4110 Households
  - 4120 Other
- 4200 Recurrent net wealth taxes
  - 4210 Individuals
  - 4220 Corporates
- 4300 Estate, inheritance and gift taxes
  - 4310 Estate and inheritance taxes
  - 4320 Gift taxes
- 4400 Taxes on financial and capital transactions
- 4500 Other non-recurrent taxes on property
- 4600 Other recurrent taxes on property

5000 *Taxes on goods and services*

- 5100 Taxes on production, sale and transfer of goods and services
  - 5110 General sales taxes
    - 5111 Value-added taxes
    - 5112 Sales taxes
    - 5113 Other general taxes
  - 5120 Taxes on specific goods and services
    - 5121 Excises
    - 5122 Profits of fiscal monopolies
    - 5123 Customs and import duties
    - 5124 On exports
    - 5125 On investment goods
    - 5126 On specific services
    - 5127 Other taxes on international trade and transactions
    - 5128 Other taxes on specific goods and services
  - 5130 Unallocable as between 5110 and 5120
- 5200 Taxes on use of goods
  - 5210 Recurrent taxes
    - 5211 Motor vehicles taxes households
    - 5212 Motor vehicles taxes others
    - 5213 Other recurrent taxes
  - 5220 Non-recurrent taxes
- 5300 Unallocable as between 5100 and 5200

6000 *Other taxes*

- 6100 Paid solely by business
- 6200 Paid by other than business, or unidentifiable

The OECD Interpretative Guide[1]

A. Coverage

General criteria

1. In the OECD classification the term "taxes" is confined to compulsory unrequited payments to general government. Taxes are unrequited in the sense that benefits provided by government to taxpayers are not normally in proportion to their payments.

2. The term 'tax' does not include fines unrelated to tax offences and compulsory loans paid to government. Borderline cases between tax and non-tax revenues in relation to certain fees and charges are discussed in §9–13.

3. General government consists of the central administration, agencies whose operations are under its effective control, state and local governments and their administrations, certain social security schemes and autonomous governmental entities, excluding public enterprises. This definition of government follows that of the 2008 *System of National Accounts* (SNA).[2] In that publication, the general government sector and its sub-sectors are defined in chapter 4, section F, pages 80-84.

4. Compulsory payments to supra-national bodies and their agencies are no longer included as taxes as from 1998, with some exceptions. However, custom duties collected by EU member states on behalf of the European Union are still identified as memorandum items and included in overall tax revenue amounts in the country tables (Part III) of the country in which they are collected. (See §95). In countries where the church forms part of general government church taxes are included, provided they meet the criteria set out in §1 above. As the data refer to receipts of general government, levies paid to non-government bodies, welfare agencies or social insurance schemes outside general government, trade unions or trade associations, even where such levies are compulsory, are excluded. Compulsory payments to general government earmarked for such bodies are, however, included, provided that the government is not simply acting in an agency capacity.[3] Profits from fiscal monopolies are distinguished from those of other public enterprises and are treated as taxes because they reflect the exercise of the taxing power of the state by the use of monopoly powers (see §62–64), as are profits received by the government from the purchase and sale of foreign exchange at different rates (see §70).

5. Taxes paid by governments (e.g. social security contributions and payroll taxes paid by governments in their capacity as an employer, consumption taxes on their purchases or taxes on their property) are not excluded from the data provided. However, where it is possible to identify the amounts of revenue involved,[4] they are shown in section III.C of this Report.

6. The relationship between this classification and that of the System of National Accounts (SNA) is set out in Sections H and J below. Because of the differences between the two classifications, the data shown in national accounts are sometimes calculated or classified differently from the practice set out in this guide. These and other differences are mentioned where appropriate (e.g. in §13 and §26 below) but it is not possible to refer to all

of them. There may also be some differences between this classification and that employed domestically by certain national administrations (e.g. see §10 below), so that OECD and national statistics data may not always be consistent: any such differences, however, are likely to be very slight in terms of amounts of revenues involved.

Social security contributions

7. Compulsory social security contributions, as defined in §35 below, paid to general government, are treated here as tax revenues. Being compulsory payments to general government they clearly resemble taxes. They may, however, differ from other taxes in that the receipt of social security benefits depends, in most countries, upon appropriate contributions having been made, although the size of the benefits is not necessarily related to the amount of the contributions. Better comparability between countries is obtained by treating social security contributions as taxes, but they are listed under a separate heading so that they can be distinguished in any analysis.

8. Social security contributions which are either voluntary or not payable to general government (see §1) are not treated as taxes, though in some countries, as indicated in the country footnotes, there are difficulties in eliminating voluntary contributions and certain compulsory payments to the private sector.

Fees, user charges and licence fees

9. Apart from vehicle licence fees, which are universally regarded as taxes, it is not easy to distinguish between those fees and user charges which are to be treated as taxes and those which are not, since, whilst a fee or charge is levied in connection with a specific service or activity, the strength of the link between the fee and the service provided may vary considerably, as may the relation between the amount of the fee and the cost of providing the service. Where the recipient of a service pays a fee clearly related to the cost of providing the service, the levy may be regarded as requited and under the definition of §1 would not be considered as a tax. In the following cases, however, a levy could be considered as 'unrequited':

a) where the charge greatly exceeds the cost of providing the service;

b) where the payer of the levy is not the receiver of the benefit (e.g. a fee collected from slaughterhouses to finance a service which is provided to farmers);

c) where government is not providing a specific service in return for the levy which it receives even though a licence may be issued to the payer (e.g. where the government grants a hunting, fishing or shooting licence which is not accompanied by the right to use a specific area of government land);

d) where benefits are received only by those paying the levy but the benefits received by each individual are not necessarily in proportion to his payments (e.g. a milk marketing levy paid by dairy farmers and used to promote the consumption of milk).

10. In marginal cases, however, the application of the criteria set out in §1 can be particularly difficult. The solution adopted – given the desirability of international uniformity and the relatively small amounts of revenue usually involved – is to follow the predominant practice among tax administrations rather than to allow each country to adopt its own view as to whether such levies are regarded as taxes or as non-tax revenue.[5]

11. A list of the main fees and charges in question and their normal[6] treatment in this publication is as follows:

Non-tax revenues:	court fees; driving licence fees; harbour fees; passport fees; radio and television licence fees where public authorities provide the service.
Taxes within heading 5200:	permission to perform such activities as distributing films; hunting, fishing and shooting; providing entertainment or gambling facilities; selling alcohol or tobacco; permission to own dogs or to use or own motor vehicles or guns; severance taxes.

12. In practice it may not always be possible to isolate tax receipts from non-tax revenue receipts when they are recorded together. If it is estimated that the bulk of the receipts derive from non-tax revenues, the whole amount involved is treated as a non-tax revenue; otherwise, such government receipts are included and classified according to the rules provided in §28 below.

13. Two differences between the OECD classification and SNA regarding the borderline between tax and non-tax revenues are:

a) SNA classifies a number of levies as indirect taxes if paid by enterprises, but as non-tax revenues if paid by households, a distinction which is regarded as irrelevant in this classification for distinguishing between tax and non-tax revenues.[7]

b) Predominant practice among most OECD tax administrations, which is occasionally used in this classification for distinguishing between tax and non-tax revenues, is not a relevant criterion for SNA purposes.

Royalties

14. Royalty payments for the right to extract oil and gas or to exploit other mineral resources are normally regarded as non-tax revenues since they are property income from government-owned land or resources.

Fines and penalties

15. Receipts from fines and penalties paid for infringement of regulations identified as relating to a particular tax and interest on payments overdue in respect of a particular tax are recorded together with receipts from that tax. Other kinds of fines identifiable as relating to tax offences are classified in the residual heading 6000. Fines not relating to tax offences (e.g. for parking offences), or not identifiable as relating to tax offences, are not treated as taxes.

B. Basis of reporting

Accrual reporting

16. The data reported in this publication for recent years are predominantly recorded on an accrual basis, i.e. recorded at the time that the tax liability was created. Further information is provided in the footnotes to the country table in Part III of the Report.

17. However, data for earlier years are still predominantly recorded on a cash basis, i.e. at the time at which the payment was received by government. Thus, for example, taxes

withheld by employers in one year but paid to the government in the following year and taxes due in one year but actually paid in the following year are both included in the receipts of the second year. Corrective transactions, such as refunds, repayments and drawbacks, are deducted from gross revenues of the period in which they are made.

18. Data on tax revenues are recorded without offsets for the administrative expenses connected with tax collection. Similarly, where the proceeds of tax are used to subsidise particular members of the community, the subsidy is not deducted from the yield of the tax, though the tax may be shown net of subsidies in the national records of some countries.

19. As regards fiscal monopolies (heading 5122), only the amount actually transferred to the government is included in government revenues. However, if any expenditures of fiscal monopolies are considered to be government expenditures (e.g. social expenditures undertaken by fiscal monopolies at the direction of the government) they are added back for the purpose of arriving at tax revenue figures (see §62 below).

The distinction between tax and expenditure provisions[8]

20. Because this publication is concerned only with the revenue side of government operations, no account being taken of the expenditure side, a distinction has to be made between tax and expenditure provisions. Normally there is no difficulty in making this distinction as expenditures are made outside the tax system and the tax accounts and under legislation separate from the tax legislation. In borderline cases, cash flow is used to distinguish between tax provisions and expenditure provisions. Insofar as a provision affects the flow of tax payments from the taxpayer to the government, it is regarded as a tax provision and is taken into account in the data shown in this publication. A provision which does not affect this flow is seen as an expenditure provision and is disregarded in the data recorded in this publication.

21. Tax allowances, exemptions and deductions against the tax base clearly affect the amount of tax paid to the government and are therefore considered as tax provisions. At the other extreme, those subsidies which cannot be offset against tax liability and which are clearly not connected with the assessment process, do not reduce tax revenues as recorded in this publication. Tax credits are amounts deductible from tax payable (as distinct from deductions from the tax base). Two types of tax credits are distinguished, those (referred to here as wastable tax credits) which are limited to the amount of the tax liability and therefore cannot give rise to a payment by the authorities to the taxpayer, and those (referred to as non-wastable tax credits) which are not so limited, so that the excess of the credit over the tax liability can be paid to the taxpayer.[9] A wastable tax credit, like a tax allowance, clearly affects the amount of tax paid to the government, and is therefore considered as a tax provision. The practice followed for non-wastable tax credits[10] is to distinguish between the 'tax expenditure component',[11] which is that portion of the credit that is used to reduce or eliminate a taxpayer's liability, and the 'transfer component', which is the portion that exceeds the taxpayer's liability and is paid to that taxpayer. Reported tax revenues should be reduced by the amount of the tax expenditure component but not by the amount of the transfer component. In addition, the amounts of the tax expenditure and transfer components should be reported as memorandum items in the country tables. Countries that are unable to distinguish between the tax expenditure and transfer components should indicate whether or not the tax revenues have been reduced by the total of these components, and provide any available estimates of the amounts of the two components. Further information is given in section C of Part I of the Report, which illustrates the effect of alternative treatments of non-wastable tax credits on Tax to GDP.

Calendar and fiscal years

22. National authorities whose fiscal years do not correspond to the calendar year show data, where possible, on a calendar year basis to permit maximum comparability with the data of other countries. There remain a few countries where data refer to fiscal years. For these the GDP data used in the comparative tables also correspond to the fiscal years.

C. General classification criteria

The main classification criteria

23. The classification of receipts among the main headings (1000, 2000, 3000, 4000, 5000 and 6000) is generally governed by the base on which the tax is levied: 1000 income, profits and capital gains; 2000 and 3000 earnings, payroll or number of employees; 4000 property; 5000 goods and services; 6000 multiple bases, other bases or unidentifiable bases. Where a tax is calculated on more than one base, the receipts are, where possible, split among the various headings (see §28 and §78). The headings 4000 and 5000 cover not only taxes where the tax base is the property, goods or services themselves but also certain related taxes. Thus, taxes on the transfer of property are included in 4400[12] and taxes on the use of goods or on permission to perform activities in 5200. In headings 4000 and 5000 a distinction is made in certain sub-headings between recurrent and non-recurrent taxes: recurrent taxes are defined as those levied at regular intervals (usually annually) and non-recurrent taxes are levied once and for all (see also §43 to §46, §49, §50 and §76 for particular applications of this distinction).

24. Earmarking of a tax for specific purposes does not affect the classification of tax receipts. However, as explained in §35 on the classification of social security contributions, the conferment of an entitlement to social benefits is crucial to the definition of the 2000 main heading.

25. The way that a tax is levied or collected (e.g. by use of stamps) does not affect classification.

Classification of taxpayers

26. In certain sub-headings distinctions are made between different categories of taxpayers. These distinctions vary from tax to tax:

a) Between individuals and corporations in relation to income and net wealth taxes

The basic distinction is that corporation income taxes, as distinct from individual income taxes, are levied on the corporation as an entity, not on the individuals who own it, and without regard to the personal circumstances of these individuals. The same distinction applies to net wealth taxes on corporations and those on individuals. Taxes paid on the profits of partnerships and the income of institutions, such as life insurance or pension funds, are classified according to the same rule. They are classified as corporate taxes (1200) if they are charged on the partnership or institution as an entity without regard to the personal circumstances of the owners. Otherwise, they are treated as individual taxes (1100). Usually, there is different legislation for the corporation taxes and for the individual taxes.[13] The distinction made here between individuals and corporations does not follow the sector classification between households, enterprises, and so on of the System of National Accounts for income and outlay accounts. The SNA classification requires certain unincorporated businesses[14] to be excluded from the household sector and included with non-financial enterprises and financial institutions. The tax on the profits of these businesses, however, cannot always be separated from the tax on the other income of their owners, or can be separated only on an arbitrary basis. No attempt at this separation is made here and the whole of the individual income tax is shown together without regard to the nature of the income chargeable.

b) Between households and others in relation to taxes on immovable property

Here the distinction is that adopted by the SNA for the production and consumption expenditure accounts. The distinction is between households as consumers (i.e. excluding non-incorporated business) on the one hand and producers on the other hand. However, taxes on dwellings occupied by households, whether paid by owner-occupiers, tenants or landlords, are classified under households. This follows the common distinction made between taxes on domestic property versus taxes on business property. Some countries are not, however, in a position to make this distinction.

c) Between households and others in relation to motor vehicle licences

Here the distinction is between households as consumers on the one hand and producers on the other, as in the production and consumption expenditure accounts of the SNA.

d) Between business and others in relation to the residual taxes (6000)

The distinction is the same as in c) above between producers on the one hand and households as consumers on the other hand. Taxes which are included under the heading 6000 because they involve more than one tax base or because the tax base does not fall within any of the previous categories but which are identifiable as levyable only on producers and not on households are included under 'business'. The rest of the taxes which are included under the heading 6000 are shown as 'other' or non-identified.

Surcharges

27. Receipts from surcharges in respect of particular taxes are usually classified with the receipts from the relevant tax whether or not the surcharge is temporary. If, however, the surcharge has a characteristic which would render it classifiable in a different heading of the OECD list, receipts from the surcharge are classified under that heading separately from the relevant tax.

Unidentifiable tax receipts and residual sub-headings

28. A number of cases arise where taxes cannot be identified as belonging entirely to a heading or sub-heading of the OECD classification and the following practices are applied in such cases:

a) The heading is known, but it is not known how receipts should be allocated between sub-headings: receipts are classified in the appropriate residual sub-heading (1300, 2400, 4520, 4600, 5130, 5300 or 6200).

b) It is known that the bulk of receipts from a group of taxes (usually local taxes) is derived from taxes within a particular heading or sub-heading, but some of the taxes in the group whose amount cannot be precisely ascertained may be classifiable in other headings or sub-headings: receipts are shown in the heading or sub-heading under which most of the receipts fall.

c) Neither the heading nor sub-heading of a tax (usually local) can be identified: the tax is classified in 6200 unless it is known that it is a tax on business in which case it is classified in 6100.

D. Commentaries on items of the list

1000 – *Taxes on income, profits and capital gains*

29. This heading covers taxes levied on the net income or profits (i.e. gross income minus allowable tax reliefs) of individuals and enterprises. Also covered are taxes levied on the capital gains of individuals and enterprises, and gains from gambling.

30. Included in the heading are:

a) taxes levied predominantly on income or profits, though partially on other bases. Taxes on various bases which are not predominantly income or profits are classified according to the principles laid down in §28 and §78;

b) taxes on property, which are levied on a presumed or estimated income as part of an income tax (see also §43(a), (c) and (d));

c) compulsory payments to social security fund contributions that are levied on income but do not confer an entitlement to social benefits. When such contributions do confer an entitlement to social benefits, they are included in heading 2000 (see §35);

d) receipts from integrated scheduler income tax systems are classified as a whole in this heading, even though certain of the scheduler taxes may be based upon gross income and may not take into account the personal circumstances of the taxpayer.

31. The main subdivision of this heading is between levies on individuals (1100) and those on corporate enterprises (1200). Under each subdivision a distinction is made between taxes on income and profits (1110 and 1210), and taxes on capital gains (1120 and 1220). If certain receipts cannot be identified as appropriate to either 1100 or 1200, or if in practice this distinction cannot be made (e.g., because there are no reliable data on the recipients of payments from which withholding taxes are deducted) they are classified in 1300 as not-allocable.

Treatment of credits under imputation systems

32. Under imputation systems of corporate income tax, a company's shareholders are wholly or partly relieved of their liability to income tax on dividends paid by the company out of income or profits liable to corporate income tax. In countries with such systems,[15] part of the tax on the company's profits is available to provide relief against the shareholders' own tax liability. The relief to the shareholder takes the form of a tax credit, the amount of which may be less than, equal to, or more than the shareholder's overall tax liability. If the tax credit exceeds this tax liability the excess may be payable to the shareholder. As this type of tax credit is an integral part of the imputation system of corporate income tax, any payment to the shareholders is treated as a repayment of tax and not as expenditure (compare the treatment of other tax credits described in §21).

33. As the tax credit under imputation systems (even when exceeding tax liability) is to be regarded as a tax provision, the question arises whether it should be deducted from individual income tax receipts (1110) or corporate income tax receipts (1210). In this Report, the full amount of corporate income tax paid is shown under 1210 and no imputed

tax is included under 1110. Thus, the full amount of the credit reduces the amount of 1110 whether the credit results in a reduction of personal income tax liability or whether an actual refund is made because the credit exceeds the income tax liability. (Where, however, such tax credits are deducted from corporation tax in respect of dividends paid to corporations the amounts are deducted from the receipts of 1210.)

1120 and 1220 – *Taxes on capital gains*

34. These sub-headings comprise taxes imposed on capital gains, 1120 covering those levied on the gains of individuals and 1220 those levied on the gains of corporate enterprises, where receipts from such taxes can be separately identified. In many countries this is not the case and the receipts from such taxes are then classified with those from the income tax. Heading 1120 also includes taxes on gains from gambling.

2000 – *Social security contributions*

35. Classified here are all compulsory payments that confer an entitlement to receive a (contingent) future social benefit. Such payments are usually earmarked to finance social benefits and are often paid to institutions of general government that provide such benefits. However, such earmarking is not part of the definition of social security contributions and is not required for a tax to be classified here. However, conferment of an entitlement is required for a tax to be classified under this heading. So, levies on income or payroll that are earmarked for social security funds but do not confer an entitlement to benefit are excluded from this heading and shown under personal income taxes (1100) or taxes on payroll and workforce (3000). Taxes on other bases, such as goods and services, which are earmarked for social security benefits are not shown here but are classified according to their respective bases because they generally confer no entitlement to social security benefits.

36. Contributions for the following types of social security benefits would, *inter alia*, be included: unemployment insurance benefits and supplements, accident, injury and sickness benefits, old-age, disability and survivors' pensions, family allowances, reimbursements for medical and hospital expenses or provision of hospital or medical services. Contributions may be levied on both employees and employers.

37. Contributions may be based on earnings or payroll ('on a payroll basis') or on net income after deductions and exemptions for personal circumstances ('on an income tax basis'), and the revenues from the two bases should be separately identified if possible. However, where contributions to a general social security scheme are on a payroll basis, but the contributions of particular groups (such as the self-employed) cannot be assessed on this basis and net income is used as a proxy for gross earnings, the receipts may still be classified as being on a payroll basis. In principle, this heading excludes voluntary contributions paid to social security schemes. When separately identifiable these are shown in the memorandum item on the financing of social security benefits. In practice, however, they cannot always be separately identified from compulsory contributions, in which case they are included in this heading.

38. Contributions to social insurance schemes which are not institutions of general government and to other types of insurance schemes, provident funds, pension funds, friendly societies or other saving schemes are not considered as social security contributions. Provident funds are arrangements under which the contributions of each employee and of the corresponding employer on his/her behalf are kept in a separate account earning interest and withdrawable under specific circumstances. Pension funds are separately organised schemes negotiated between employees and employers and carry provisions for different contributions and benefits, sometimes more directly tied to salary levels and length of

service than under social security schemes. When contributions to these schemes are compulsory or quasi-compulsory (e.g. by virtue of agreement with professional and union organisations) they are shown in the memorandum item (refer to Section III.B of the Report).

39. Contributions by government employees and by governments in respect of their employees, to social security schemes classified within general government are included in this heading. Contributions to separate schemes for government employees, which can be regarded as replacing general social security schemes, are also regarded as taxes.[16] Where, however, a separate scheme is not seen as replacing a general scheme and has been negotiated between the government, in its role as an employer, and its employees, it is not regarded as social security and contributions to it are not regarded as taxes, even though the scheme may have been established by legislation.

40. This heading excludes 'imputed' contributions, which correspond to social benefits paid directly by employers to their employees or former employees or to their representatives (e.g. when employers are legally obliged to pay sickness benefits for a certain period).

41. Contributions are divided into those of employees (2100), employers (2200), and self-employed or non-employed (2300), and then further sub-divided according to the basis on which they are levied. Employees are defined for this purpose as all persons engaged in activities of business units, government bodies, private non-profit institutions, or other paid employment, except the proprietors and their unpaid family members in the case of unincorporated businesses. Members of the armed forces are included, irrespective of the duration and type of their service, if they contribute to social security schemes. The contributions of employers are defined as their payments on account of their employees to social security schemes. Where employees or employers are required to continue the payment of social security contributions when the employee becomes unemployed these contributions, data permitting, are shown in 2100 and 2200 respectively. Accordingly, the sub-heading 2300 is confined to contributions paid by the self-employed and by those outside of the labour force (e.g. disabled or retired individuals).

3000 – ***Taxes on payroll and workforce***

42. This heading covers taxes paid by employers, employees or the self-employed either as a proportion of payroll or as a fixed amount per person, and which do not confer entitlement to social benefits. Examples of taxes classified here are the United Kingdom national insurance surcharge (introduced in 1977), the Swedish payroll tax (1969–1979), and the Austrian Contribution to the Family Burden Equalisation Fund and Community Tax.

4000 – ***Taxes on property***

43. This heading covers recurrent and non-recurrent taxes on the use, ownership or transfer of property. These include taxes on immovable property or net wealth, taxes on the change of ownership of property through inheritance or gift and taxes on financial and capital transactions. The following kinds of tax are excluded from this heading:

a) taxes on capital gains resulting from the sale of a property (1120 or 1220);

b) taxes on the use of goods or on permission to use goods or perform activities (5200); see §73;

c) taxes on immovable property levied on the basis of a presumed net income which take into account the personal circumstances of the taxpayer. They are classified as income taxes along with taxes on income and capital gains derived from property (1100);

d) taxes on the use of property for residence, where the tax is payable by either proprietor or tenant and the amount payable is a function of the user's personal circumstances (pay, dependants, and so on). They are classified as taxes on income (1100);

e) taxes on building in excess of permitted maximum density, taxes on the enlargement, construction or alteration of certain buildings beyond a permitted value and taxes on building construction. They are classified as taxes on permission to perform activities (5200);

f) taxes on the use of one's own property for special trading purposes like selling alcohol, tobacco, meat or for exploitation of land resources (e.g., United States severance taxes). They are classified as taxes on permission to perform activities (5200).

4100 – *Recurrent taxes on immovable property*

44. This sub-heading covers taxes levied regularly in respect of the use or ownership of immovable property.

- these taxes are levied on land and buildings;
- they can be in the form of a percentage of an assessed property value based on a national rental income, sales price, or capitalised yield; or in terms of other characteristics of real property, (for example size or location) from which a presumed rent or capital value can be derived.
- such taxes can be levied on proprietors, tenants, or both. They can also be paid by one level of government to another level of government in respect of property under the jurisdiction of the latter.
- debts are not taken into account in the assessment of these taxes, and they differ from taxes on net wealth in this respect.

45. Taxes on immovable property are further sub-divided into those paid by households (4110) and those paid by other entities (4120), according to the criteria set out in §26(*b*) above.

4200 – *Recurrent taxes on net wealth*

46. This sub-heading covers taxes levied regularly (in most cases annually) on net wealth, i.e. taxes on a wide range of movable and immovable property, net of debt. It is sub-divided into taxes paid by individuals (4210) and taxes paid by corporate enterprises (4220) according to the criteria set out in §26(*a*) above. If separate figures exist for receipts paid by institutions, the tax payments involved are added to those paid by corporations.

4300 – *Estate, inheritance and gift taxes*

47. This sub-heading is divided into taxes on estates and inheritances (4310) and taxes on gifts (4320).[17] Estate taxes are charged on the amount of the total estate whereas inheritance taxes are charged on the shares of the individual recipients; in addition the latter may take into account the relationship of the individual recipients to the deceased.

4400 – *Taxes on financial and capital transactions*

48. This sub-heading comprises, *inter alia*, taxes on the issue, transfer, purchase and sale of securities, taxes on cheques, and taxes levied on specific legal transactions such as validation of contracts and the sale of immovable property. The heading does not include:

a) taxes on the use of goods or property or permission to perform certain activities (5200);

b) fees paid to cover court charges, charges for birth, marriage or death certificates, which are normally regarded as non-tax revenues (see §9);

c) taxes on capital gains (1000);

d) recurrent taxes on immovable property (4100);

e) recurrent taxes on net wealth (4200);

f) once-and-for-all levies on property or wealth (4500).

4500 – *Other non-recurrent taxes on property*[16]

49. This sub-heading covers once-and-for-all, as distinct from recurrent, levies on property. It is divided into taxes on net wealth (4510) and other non-recurrent taxes on property (4520). Heading 4510 would include taxes levied to meet emergency expenditures, or for redistribution purposes. Heading 4520 would cover taxes levied to take account of increases in land value due to permission given to develop or provision of additional local facilities by general government, any taxes on the revaluation of capital and once-and-for-all taxes on particular items of property.

4600 – *Other recurrent taxes on property*

50. These rarely exist in OECD member countries, but the heading would include taxes on goods such as cattle, jewellery, windows, and other external signs of wealth.

5000 – *Taxes on goods and services*

51. All taxes and duties levied on the production, extraction, sale, transfer, leasing or delivery of goods, and the rendering of services (5100), or in respect of the use of goods or permission to use goods or to perform activities (5200) are included here. The heading thus covers:

a) multi-stage cumulative taxes;

b) general sales taxes – whether levied at manufacture/production, wholesale or retail level;

c) value-added taxes;

d) excises;

e) taxes levied on the import and export of goods;

f) taxes levied in respect of the use of goods and taxes on permission to use goods, or perform certain activities;

g) taxes on the extraction, processing or production of minerals and other products.

52. Borderline cases between this heading and heading 4000 (taxes on property) and 6100 (other taxes on business) are referred to in §43, §48 and §75. Residual sub-headings (5300) and (5130) cover tax receipts which cannot be allocated between 5100 and 5200 and between 5110 and 5120, respectively; see §28.

5100 – *Taxes on the production, sale, transfer, leasing and delivery of goods and rendering of services*

53. This sub-heading consists of all taxes, levied on transactions in goods and services on the basis of their intrinsic characteristics (e.g. value, weight of tobacco, strength of alcohol, and so on) as distinct from taxes imposed on the use of goods, or permission to use goods or perform activities, which fall under 5200.

5110 – *General taxes on goods and services*

54. This sub-heading includes all taxes, other than import and export duties (5123 and 5124), levied on the production, leasing, transfer, delivery or sales of a wide range of goods and/or the rendering of a wide range of services, irrespective of whether they are domestically produced or imported and irrespective of the stage of production or distribution at which they are levied. It thus covers value-added taxes, sales taxes and multi-stage cumulative taxes. Receipts from border adjustments in respect of such taxes when goods are imported are added to gross receipts for this category, and repayments of such taxes when goods are exported are deducted. These taxes are subdivided into 5111 value-added taxes, 5112 sales taxes, 5113 other general taxes on goods and services.

55. Borderline cases arise between this heading and taxes on specific goods (5120) when taxes are levied on a large number of goods, for example, the United Kingdom purchase tax (repealed in 1973) and the Japanese commodity tax (repealed in 1988). In conformity with national views, the former United Kingdom purchase tax is classified as a general tax (5112) and the former Japanese commodity tax as excises (5121).

5111 – *Value-added taxes*

56. All general consumption taxes charged on value-added are classified in this sub-heading, irrespective of the method of deduction and the stages at which the taxes are levied. In practice, all OECD countries with value-added taxes normally allow immediate deduction of taxes on purchases by all but the final consumer and impose tax at all stages. In some countries the heading may include certain taxes, such as those on financial and insurance activities, either because receipts from them cannot be identified separately from those from the value-added tax, or because they are regarded as an integral part of the value-added tax, even though similar taxes in other countries might be classified elsewhere (e.g. 5126 as taxes on services or 4400 as taxes on financial and capital transactions).

5112 – *Sales taxes*

57. All general taxes levied at one stage only, whether at manufacturing or production, wholesale or retail stage are classified here.

5113 – *Other general taxes on goods and services*

58. This sub-heading covers multi-stage cumulative taxes (also known as 'cascade taxes') where tax is levied each time a transaction takes place without deduction for tax paid on inputs, and also those general consumption taxes where elements of value-added, sales or cascade taxes are combined.

5120 – *Taxes on specific goods and services*

59. Excises, profits generated and transferred from fiscal monopolies, and customs and imports duties as well as taxes on exports, foreign exchange transactions, investment goods and betting stakes and special taxes on services, which do not form part of a general tax of 5110, are included in this category.

5121 – *Excises*

60. Excises are taxes levied on particular products, or on a limited range of products, which are not classifiable under 5110 (general taxes), 5123 (import duties) and 5124 (export duties). They may be imposed at any stage of production or distribution and are usually assessed by reference to the weight or strength or quantity of the product, but sometimes by reference to value. Thus, special taxes on, for example, sugar, beetroot, matches, chocolates, and taxes at varying rates on a certain range of goods, as well as those levied in most countries on tobacco goods, alcoholic drinks and hydrocarbon oils and other energy sources, are included in this sub-heading.

61. Excises are distinguished from:

a) 5110 (general taxes). This is discussed in §54-55;

b) 5123 (import duties). If a tax collected principally on imported goods also applies, or would apply, under the law by which the tax is imposed to comparable home-produced goods, the receipts there from would be classified as excises (5121). This principle applies even if there is no comparable home production or no possibility of it (see also §65);

c) 5126 (taxes on services). The problem here arises in respect of taxes on electricity, gas and energy. All of these are regarded as taxes on goods and are included under 5121.

5122 – *Profits of fiscal monopolies*

62. This sub-heading covers that part of the profits of fiscal monopolies which is transferred to general government or which is used to finance any expenditures considered to be government expenditures (see §19). Amounts are shown when they are transferred to general government or used to make expenditures considered to be government expenditures

63. Fiscal monopolies reflect the exercise of the taxing power of government by the use of monopoly powers. Fiscal monopolies are non-financial public enterprises exercising a monopoly in most cases over the production or distribution of tobacco, alcoholic beverages, salt, matches, playing cards and petroleum or agricultural products (i.e. on the kind of products which are likely to be, alternatively or additionally, subject to the excises of 5121), to raise the government revenues which in other countries are gathered through taxes on dealings in such commodities by private business units. The government monopoly may be at the production stage or, as in the case of government-owned and controlled liquor stores, at the distribution stage.

64. Fiscal monopolies are distinguished from public utilities such as rail transport, electricity, post offices, and other communications, which may enjoy a monopoly or quasi-monopoly position but where the primary purpose is normally to provide basic services rather than to raise revenue for government. Transfers from such other public enterprises to the government are considered as non-tax revenues. The traditional concept of fiscal monopoly has not been extended to include state lotteries, the profits of which are accordingly regarded as non-tax revenues. Fiscal monopoly profits are distinguished from export and import monopoly profits (5127) transferred from marketing boards or other enterprises dealing with international trade.

5123 – *Customs and other import duties*

65. Taxes, stamp duties and surcharges restricted by law to imported products are included here. Also included are levies on imported agricultural products which are imposed in

member countries of the European Union and amounts paid by certain of these countries under the Monetary Compensation Accounts (MCA) system.[18] Starting from 1998, customs duties collected by European Union member states on behalf of the European Union are no longer reported under this heading in the country tables (in Part III of the Report). Excluded here are taxes collected on imports as part of a general tax on goods and services, or an excise applicable to both imported and domestically produced goods.

5124 – *Taxes on exports*

66. In the 1970s, export duties were levied in Australia, Canada and Portugal as a regular measure and they have been used in Finland for counter-cyclical purposes. Some member countries of the European Union pay, as part of the MCA system, a levy on exports (see note 18 to §65). Where these amounts are identifiable, they are shown in this heading. This heading does not include repayments of general consumption taxes or excises or customs duties on exported goods, which should be deducted from the gross receipts under 5110, 5121 or 5123, as appropriate.

5125 – *Taxes on investment goods*

67. This sub-heading covers taxes on investment goods, such as machinery. These taxes may be imposed for a number of years or temporarily for counter-cyclical purposes. Taxes on industrial inputs which are also levied on consumers [e.g. the Swedish energy tax which is classified under (5121)] are not included here.

5126 – *Taxes on specific services*

68. All taxes assessed on the payment for specific services, such as taxes on insurance premiums, banking services, gambling and betting stakes (e.g. from horse races, football pools, lottery tickets), transport, entertainment, restaurant and advertising charges, fall into this category. Taxes levied on the gross income of companies providing the service (e.g. gross insurance premiums or gambling stakes received by the company) are also classified under this heading. Tax revenues from bank levies and payments to deposit insurance and financial stability schemes are provisionally included here for the 2012 edition. The detailed classification is set out in paragraph 105.

69. Excluded from this sub-heading are:

a) taxes on services forming part of a general tax on goods and services (5110);

b) taxes on electricity, gas and energy (5121 as excises);

c) taxes on individual gains from gambling (1120 as taxes on capital gains of individuals and non-corporate enterprises) and lump-sum taxes on the transfer of private lotteries or on the permission to set up lotteries (5200);[19]

d) taxes on cheques and on the issue, transfer or redemption of securities (4400 as taxes on financial and capital transactions).

5127 – *Other taxes on international trade and transactions*

70. This sub-heading covers revenue received by the government from the purchase and sale of foreign exchange at different rates. When the government exercises monopoly powers to extract a margin between the purchase and sales price of foreign exchange, other than to cover administrative costs, the revenue derived constitutes a compulsory levy exacted in indeterminate proportions from both purchaser and seller of foreign exchange. It is the common equivalent of an import duty and export duty levied in a single exchange rate system or of a tax on the sale or purchase of foreign exchange. Like the profits of fiscal

monopolies and import or export monopolies transferred to government, it represents the exercise of monopoly powers for tax purposes and is included in tax revenues.

71. The sub-heading covers also the profits of export or import monopolies, which do not however exist in OECD countries, taxes on purchase or sale of foreign exchange, and any other taxes levied specifically on international trade or transactions.

5128 – *Other taxes on specific goods and services*

72. This item includes taxes on the extraction of minerals, fossil fuels and other exhaustible resources from deposits owned privately or by another government together with any other unidentifiable receipts from taxes on specific goods and services. Taxes on the extraction of exhaustible resources are usually a fixed amount per unit of quality or weight, but can be a percentage of value. The taxes are recorded when the resources are extracted. Payments from the extraction of exhaustible resources from deposits owned by the government unit receiving the payment are classified as rent.

5200 – *Taxes on use of goods or on permission to use goods or perform activities*

73. This sub-heading covers taxes which are levied in respect of the use of goods as distinct from taxes on the goods themselves. Unlike the latter taxes – reported under 5100 –, they are not assessed on the value of the goods but usually as fixed amounts. Taxes on permission to use goods or to perform activities are also included here, as are pollution taxes not based upon the value of particular goods. It is sometimes difficult to distinguish between compulsory user charges and licence fees which are regarded as taxes and those which are excluded as non-tax revenues. The criteria which are employed are noted in §9–10.

74. Although the sub-heading refers to the 'use' of goods, registration of ownership rather than use may be what generates liability to tax, so that the taxes of this heading may apply to the ownership of animals or goods rather than their use (e.g. race horses, dogs and motor vehicles) and may apply even to unusable goods (e.g. unusable motor vehicles or guns).

75. Borderline cases arise with:

a) taxes on the permission to perform business activities which are levied on a combined income, payroll or turnover base and, accordingly, are classified following the rules in §78;

b) taxes on the ownership or use of property of headings 4100, 4200 and 4600. The heading 4100 is confined to taxes on the ownership or tenancy of immovable property and – unlike the taxes of 5200 – they are related to the value of the property. The net wealth taxes and taxes on chattels of 4200 and 4600 respectively are confined to the ownership rather than the use of assets, apply to groups of assets rather than particular goods and again are related to the value of the assets

5210 – *Recurrent taxes on use of goods and on permission to use goods or perform activities*

76. The principal characteristic of taxes classified here is that they are levied at regular intervals and that they are usually fixed amounts. The most important item in terms of revenue receipts is vehicle licence taxes. This sub-heading also covers taxes on permission to hunt, shoot, fish or to sell certain products and taxes on the ownership of dogs and on the performance of certain services, provided that they meet the criteria set out in §9–10. The sub-divisions of 5210 are user taxes on motor vehicles paid by households (5211) and those paid by others (5212).[20] Sub-heading 5213 covers dog licences and user charges for

permission to perform activities such as selling meat or liquor when the levies are on a recurring basis. It also covers recurrent general licences for hunting, shooting and fishing where the right to carry out these activities is not granted as part of a normal commercial transaction (e.g. the granting of the licence is not accompanied by the right to use a specific area which is owned by government).

5220 – *Non-recurrent taxes on use of goods and on permission to use goods or perform activities*

77. This section covers non-recurrent taxes levied on the use of goods or on permission to use goods or perform activities and taxes levied each time goods are used. It includes taxes levied on the emission or discharge into the environment of noxious gases, liquids or other harmful substances.

- Payments for tradable emission permits issued by governments under cap and trade schemes should be recorded here at the time the emissions occur. No revenue should be recorded for permits that governments issue free of charge. The accrual basis of recording means that there can be a timing difference between the cash being received by government for the permits and the time the emission occurs. In the national accounts, this timing gives rise to a financial liability for government during the period.

- Payments made for the collection and disposal of waste or noxious substances by public authorities should be excluded as they constitute a sale of services to enterprises.

78. Other taxes falling under heading 5200 that are not levied recurrently are also included here. Thus, once-and-for-all payments for permission to sell liquor or tobacco or to set up betting shops are included provided they meet the criteria set out in §9–10.

6000 – *Other taxes*

79. Taxes levied on a base, or bases, other than those described under headings 1000, 3000, 4000 and 5000, or on bases of which none could be regarded as being predominantly the same as that of any one of these headings, are covered here. As regards taxes levied on a multiple base, if it is possible to estimate receipts related to each base (e.g. the Austrian and German 'Gewerbesteuer') this is done and the separate amounts included under the appropriate headings. If the separate amounts cannot be estimated, but it is known that most of the receipts are derived from one base, the whole of the receipts are classified according to that base. If neither of these procedures can be followed, they are classified here. The sub-headings may also include receipts from taxes which governments are unable to identify or isolate (see §28). Included here also are fines and penalties paid for infringement of regulations relating to taxes but not identifiable as relating to a particular category of taxes (see §15). A subdivision is made between taxes levied wholly or predominantly on business (6100) and those levied on others (6200).

E. Conciliation with National Accounts

80. This section of the tables provides a re-conciliation between the OECD calculation of total tax revenues and the total of all taxes and social contributions paid to general government as recorded in the country's National Accounts. Where the country is a member of the European Union (EU), the comparison is between the OECD calculation of total tax

revenues and the sum of tax revenues and social contributions recorded in the combination of the general government and the institutions of the EU sectors of the National Accounts.

F. Memorandum item on the financing of social security benefits

81. In view of the varying relationship between taxation and social security contributions and the cases referred to in §35 to §41, a memorandum item collects together all payments earmarked for social security-type benefits, other than voluntary payments to the private sector. Data are presented as follows (refer section III.B of the Report):

a) Taxes of 2000 series.

b) Taxes earmarked for social security benefits.

c) Voluntary contributions to the government.

d) Compulsory contributions to the private sector.

Guidance on the breakdown of (a) to (d) above is provided in §35 to §41.

G. Memorandum item on identifiable taxes paid by government

82. Identifiable taxes actually paid by government are presented in a memorandum item classified by the main headings of the OECD classification of taxes. In the vast majority of countries, only social security contributions and payroll taxes paid by government can be identified. These are, however, usually the most important taxes paid by governments (refer section III.C of the Report).

H. Relation of OECD classification of taxes to national accounting systems

83. A system of national accounts (SNA) seeks to provide a coherent framework for recording and presenting the main flows relating respectively to production, consumption, accumulation and external transactions of a given economic area, usually a country or a major region within a country. Government revenues are an important part of the transactions recorded in SNA. The final version of the 2008 SNA was jointly published by five international organisations: the United Nations, the International Monetary Fund, the European Union, the Organisation for Economic Co-operation and Development, and the World Bank in August 2009. The *System* is a comprehensive, consistent and flexible set of macroeconomic accounts. It is designed for use in countries with market economies, whatever their stage of economic development, and also in countries in transition to market economies. The important parts of the SNA's conceptual framework and its definitions of the various sectors of the economy have been reflected in the OECD's classification of taxes.

84. There are, however, some differences between the OECD classification of taxes and SNA concepts that are listed below. They arise because the aim of the former is to provide the maximum disaggregation of statistical data on what are generally regarded as taxes by tax administrations.

a) OECD includes social security contributions in total tax revenues (§7 and §8 above);

b) there are different points of view on whether or not some levies and fees are classified as taxes (§9 and §10 above);

K. Attribution of tax revenues by sub-sectors of general government

89. The OECD classification requires a breakdown of tax revenues by sub-sectors of government. The definition of each sub-sector and the criteria to be used to attribute tax revenues between these sub-sectors are set out below. They follow the guidance of the 2008 SNA and GFSM2001.

Sub-sectors of general government to be identified

a) Central government

90. The central government sub-sector includes all governmental departments, offices, establishments and other bodies which are agencies or instruments of the central authority whose competence extends over the whole territory, with the exception of the administration of social security funds. Central government therefore has the authority to impose taxes on all resident and non-resident units engaged in economic activities within the country.

b) State, provincial or regional government

91. This sub-sector consists of intermediate units of government exercising a competence at a level below that of central government. It includes all such units operating independently of central government in a part of a country's territory encompassing a number of smaller localities, with the exception of the administration of social security funds. In unitary countries, regional governments may be considered to have a separate existence where they have substantial autonomy to raise a significant proportion of their revenues from sources within their control and their officers are independent of external administrative control in the actual operation of the unit's activities.

92. At present, federal countries comprise the majority of cases where revenues attributed to intermediate units of government are identified separately. Spain is the only unitary country in this position. In the remaining unitary countries, regional revenues are included with those of local governments.

c) Local government

93. This sub-sector includes all other units of government exercising an independent competence in part of the territory of a country, with the exception of the administration of social security funds. It encompasses various urban and/or rural jurisdictions (e.g. local authorities, municipalities, cities, boroughs, districts).

d) Social security funds

94. Social security funds form a separate sub-sector of general government. The social security sub-sector is defined in the 2008 SNA by the following extracts from paragraphs 4.124 to 4.126 and 4.147:

"Social security schemes are social insurance schemes covering the community as a whole or large section of the community that are imposed and controlled by government units. The schemes cover a wide variety of programmes, providing benefits in cash or in kind for old age, invalidity or death, survivors, sickness and maternity, work injury, unemployment, family allowance, health care, etc. There is not necessarily a direct link between the amount of the contribution paid by an individual and the benefits he or she may receive." (Paragraph 4.124).

"When social security schemes are separately organised from the other activities of government units and hold their assets and liabilities separately from the latter and engage in financial transactions on their own account they qualify as institutional units that are described as social security funds" (Paragraph 4.125).

"The amounts raised, and paid out, in social security contributions and benefits may be deliberately varied in order to achieve objectives of government policy that have no direct connection with the concept of social security as a scheme to provide social benefits to members of the community. They may be raised or lowered in order to influence the level of aggregate demand in the economy, for example. Nevertheless, so long as they remain separately constituted funds, they must be treated as separate institutional units in the SNA. (Paragraph 4.126)

"The social security funds sub-sector (of general government) consists of the social security funds operating at all levels of government. Such funds are social insurance schemes covering the community as a whole or large section of the community that are imposed by government units" (Paragraph 4.147).

95. This definition of social security funds is followed in the OECD classification with the two following exceptions which are excluded:

- Schemes imposed by government and operated by bodies outside the general government sector, as defined in §3 of this manual, and
- Schemes to which all contributions are voluntary.

Supra-national Authorities

96. This sub-sector covers the revenue-raising operations of supra-national authorities within a country. In practice, the only relevant supra-national authority in the OECD area is that of the institutions of the European Union (EU). As from 1998, supra-national authorities are no longer included in the *Revenue Statistics*, to achieve consistency with the SNA definition of general government which excludes them. For example, income taxes and social security contributions collected by European Institutions and paid by European civil servants who are resident of EU member countries should not be included. However the specific levies paid by the member states of the EU continue to be included in total tax revenues and they are shown under this heading.

Criteria to be used for the attribution of tax revenues

97. When a government collects taxes and pays them over in whole or in part to other governments, it is necessary to determine whether the revenues should be considered to be those of the collecting government which it distributes to others as grants, or those of the beneficiary governments which the collecting government receives and passes on only as their agent. The criteria to be used in the attribution of revenues are set out in §98 to §101 which replicate paragraphs 3.70 to 3.73 from the 2008 SNA.

98. In general, a tax is attributed to the government unit that:

a) exercises the authority to impose the tax (either as a principal or through the delegated authority of the principal);

b) has final discretion to set and vary the rate of the tax.

99. Where an amount is collected by one government for and on behalf of another government, and the latter government has the authority to impose the tax, and set and vary its rate, then the former is acting as an agent for the latter and the tax is reassigned. Any amount retained by the collecting government as a collection charge should be treated as a payment for a service. Any other amount retained by the collecting government, such as under a tax-sharing arrangement, should be treated as a current grant. If the collecting government was delegated the authority to set and vary the rate, then the amount collected should be treated as tax revenue of this government.

100. Where different governments jointly and equally set the rate of a tax and jointly and equally decide on the distribution of the proceeds, with no individual government having ultimate overriding authority, then the tax revenues are attributed to each government according to its respective share of the proceeds. If an arrangement allows one government unit to exercise ultimate overriding authority, then all of the tax revenue is attributed to that unit.

101. There may also be the circumstance where a tax is imposed under the constitutional or other authority of one government, but other governments individually set the tax rate in their jurisdictions. The proceeds of the tax generated in each respective government's jurisdiction are attributed as tax revenues of that government.

Levies paid by member states of the European Union

102. The levies paid by the member states of the EU take the form:

- VAT own resources; and
- Specific levies which include:
  - *a)* custom duties and levies on agricultural goods (5123),
  - *b)* gross monetary compensation accounts (5123 if relating to imports and 5124 if relating to exports); and
  - *c)* Steel, coal, sugar and milk levies (5128).

103. The custom duties collected by member states on behalf of the EU are recorded

- on a gross of collection fee basis
- using figures adjusted so that duties are shown on a 'final destination' as opposed to a 'country of first entry' basis where such adjustments can be made. These adjustments concern in particular duties collected at important (sea) ports. Although the EU duties are collected by the authorities of the country of first entry, when possible these duties should be excluded from the revenue of the collecting country and be included in the revenue of the country of final destination.

This is the specific EU levy that most clearly conforms to the attribution criterion described in §96 above. Consequently as from 1998, these amounts are footnoted as a memorandum item to the EU member state country tables (in Part III) and no longer shown under heading 5123. However the figures are included in the total tax revenue figures on the top line for all the relevant years shown in the tables.

104. The VAT own resources, which are determined by applying a rate not exceeding 1 per cent to an assessment basis specified in the Sixth Directive,[21] are more of a borderline case. They have some of the characteristics of a transfer (they are not derived from a clearly identifiable source of funds that are actually collected) and some of a tax (the amount of the transfer is determined by the receiving sub-sector of government). In this publication they are *not* shown as a tax of the European Union (but as a tax of the EU member states), though the amounts involved are footnoted in the tables contained in Part IV.

L. Provisional classification of revenues from bank levies and payments to deposit insurance and financial stability schemes

105. The OECD have adopted the following interim approach to reporting revenue from bank levies plus deposit insurance and stability fees for the 2012 edition of *OECD Revenue Statistics*; The amounts should be recorded under category 5126.

- Compulsory payments of stability fees, bank levies and deposit insurance should generally be treated as tax revenues where the payments are made to General Government and allocated to the governments' consolidated or general funds so that the Government is free to make immediate use of the money for the purposes that it chooses. This principle would apply regardless of whether the Government is promising to make payments to guarantee the banks' customer deposits in some future contingency.

- If the compulsory payments are made to general government and placed in funds that are earmarked to be entirely channelled back to the sector of the economy that comprises the companies that are subject to the payment, they would still generally be treated as tax revenues on the grounds that the funds would be available for the government and would reduce its budget deficit, the fee is unrequited for an individual entity and the amounts raised could be unrelated to any eventual pay out to depositors or expenditure on wider support for the financial sector.

- Payments to made to the smaller long-standing schemes for insuring 'retail' deposits, where the payment levels are consistent with the costs of insurance should be classified as fee for service.

- Any payments which involve governments realising the assets of a failed institution or receiving a priority claim on its assets in liquidation in order to fund payments of compensation to customers for their lost deposits would be treated as a fee for a service as opposed to tax revenues.

- Compulsory payments that are made to funds operated outside the government sector and non-state institutions backed by the deposit takers and all payments to voluntary schemes should not be treated as tax revenues.

Notes

1. References in the OECD Interpretative Guide to Sections or Parts of "this Report" refer to OECD(2014), *Revenue* Statistics *1965-2013,* OECD Publishing, Paris.
2. All references to SNA are to the 2008 edition.
3. See section K of this guide for a discussion of the concept of agency capacity.
4. It is usually possible to identify amounts of social security contributions and payroll taxes, but not other taxes paid by government.
5. If, however, a levy which is considered as non-tax revenue by most countries is regarded as a tax – or raises substantial revenue – in one or more countries, the amounts collected are footnoted at the end of the relevant country tables, even though the amounts are not included in total tax revenues.
6. Names, however, can frequently be misleading. For example, though a passport fee would normally be considered a non-tax revenue, if a supplementary levy on passports (as is the case in Portugal) were imposed in order to raise substantial amounts of revenue relative to the cost of providing the passport, the levy would be regarded as a tax under 5200.
7. There are practical difficulties in operating the distinction made by 1993 SNA.
8. A more detailed explanation of this distinction can be found in the special feature, 'Current issues in reporting tax revenues', in the 2001 edition of the *Revenue Statistics.*
9. Sometimes the terms 'non-refundable' and 'refundable' are used, but it may be considered illogical to talk of 'refundable' when nothing has been paid.
10. A different treatment, however, is accorded to non-wastable tax credits under imputation systems of corporate income tax (§32–34).
11. This is not strictly a true tax expenditure in the formal sense. Such tax expenditures require identification of a benchmark tax system for each country or, preferably, a common international benchmark. In practice it has not been possible to reach agreement on a common international benchmark.
12. Unless based on the profit made on a sale, in which case they would be classified as capital gains taxes under 1120 or 1220.
13. In some countries the same legislation applies to both individual and corporate enterprises for particular taxes on income. However, the receipts from such taxes are usually allocable between individuals and enterprises and can therefore be shown in the appropriate sub-heading.
14. For example, "...sufficiently self-contained and independent that they behave in the same way as corporations.......(including) keeping a complete set of accounts" (2008SNA, section 4.44).
15. In Canada – a country also referred to as having an imputation system – the (wastable) tax credit for the shareholder is in respect of domestic corporation tax deemed to have been paid whether or not a corporation tax liability has arisen. As there is no integral connection between the corporation tax liability and the credit given against income tax under such systems, these credits for dividends are treated, along with other tax credits, on the lines described in §21.
16. This may also apply where a scheme for government employees existed prior to the introduction of a general social security scheme.
17. In the 2008 SNA these are regarded as capital transfers and not as taxes (see section G).

18. This is the system by which the European Union adjusts for differences between the exchange rates used to determine prices under the Common Market Agricultural Policy and actual exchange rates. Payments under the system may relate to imports or exports and where these amounts are separately identifiable they are shown under the appropriate heading (5123 or 5124). In this Report, these amounts are shown gross (i.e. without deducting any subsidies paid out under the MCA system).

19. Transfers of profits of State lotteries are regarded as non-tax revenues (see also §64).

20. See §26(*c*) as regards this distinction.

21. At the Edinburgh Summit (1992) EU Member countries have decided to gradually reduce this percentage from 1.4 to 1, and to effectuate this reduction between years 1995 and 1999.During the period 1970–1983 this percentage also amounted to 1.

ORGANISATION FOR ECONOMIC CO-OPERATION AND DEVELOPMENT

The OECD is a unique forum where governments work together to address the economic, social and environmental challenges of globalisation. The OECD is also at the forefront of efforts to understand and to help governments respond to new developments and concerns, such as corporate governance, the information economy and the challenges of an ageing population. The Organisation provides a setting where governments can compare policy experiences, seek answers to common problems, identify good practice and work to co-ordinate domestic and international policies.

The OECD member countries are: Australia, Austria, Belgium, Canada, Chile, the Czech Republic, Denmark, Estonia, Finland, France, Germany, Greece, Hungary, Iceland, Ireland, Israel, Italy, Japan, Korea, Luxembourg, Mexico, the Netherlands, New Zealand, Norway, Poland, Portugal, the Slovak Republic, Slovenia, Spain, Sweden, Switzerland, Turkey, the United Kingdom and the United States. The European Union takes part in the work of the OECD.

OECD Publishing disseminates widely the results of the Organisation's statistics gathering and research on economic, social and environmental issues, as well as the conventions, guidelines and standards agreed by its members.

CENTRE FOR TAX POLICY AND ADMINISTRATION

The Centre for Tax Policy and Administration (CTPA) is the focal point for the OECD's work on taxation. The Centre provides technical expertise and support to the Committee on Fiscal Affairs and examines all aspects of taxation other than macro-fiscal policy. Its work covers international and domestic tax issues, direct and indirect taxes, tax policy and tax administration. CTPA also carries out an extensive global programme of dialogue between OECD and non-OECD tax officials through events held annually on the full range of OECD work, bringing together over 100 non-OECD economies. For information on the Centre for Tax Policy and Administration, please visit *www.oecd.org/tax*

OECD DEVELOPMENT CENTRE

The OECD Development Centre was established in 1962 as an independent platform for knowledge sharing and policy dialogue between OECD member countries and developing economies, allowing these countries to interact on an equal footing. Today, 27 OECD countries and 22 non-OECD countries are members of the Centre. The Centre draws attention to emerging systemic issues likely to have an impact on global development and more specific development challenges faced by today's developing and emerging economies. It uses evidence-based analysis and strategic partnerships to help countries formulate innovative policy solutions to the global challenges of development.

For more information on the Centre and its members, please see *www.oecd.org/dev*

OECD PUBLISHING, 2, rue André-Pascal, 75775 PARIS CEDEX 16
(23 2015 17 1 P) ISBN 978-92-64-23425-3 – 2015

www.ingramcontent.com/pod-product-compliance
Lightning Source LLC
LaVergne TN
LVHW081419110826
845149LV00010B/1802

* 9 7 8 9 2 6 4 2 3 4 2 5 3 *